THE SOCIAL SIGNIFICANCE
OF SPEECH

NORTH-HOLLAND
LINGUISTIC SERIES   23
Edited by S.C.DIK *and* J.G.KOOIJ

THE SOCIAL SIGNIFICANCE OF SPEECH

An Introduction to and Workbook in Sociolinquistics

John T. Platt *and* Heidi K. Platt
Department of Linquistics
Monash University
CLAYTON, Victoria
Australia

1975

NORTH-HOLLAND PUBLISHING COMPANY – AMSTERDAM • OXFORD
AMERICAN ELSEVIER PUBLISHING COMPANY, INC. – NEW YORK

North-Holland ISBN for the series: 0 7204 6180 4
North-Holland ISBN for this volume: 0 7204 6207 x
American Elsevier ISBN: 0 444 10972 2

Published by:

North-Holland Publishing Company – Amsterdam
North-Holland Publishing Company, Ltd. – Oxford

Sole distributors for the U.S.A. and Canada:

American Elsevier Publishing Company, Inc.
52 Vanderbilt Avenue
New York, N.Y. 10017

Printed in The Netherlands

Thanks are given to senior students in the
Department of Linguistics at Monash University
who gave some useful suggestions and served as
co-operative guinea pigs for many of the exercises
and assignments presented in this book.

The Singapore and Malaysia Project referred
to in various places in the book is being financed
by the Australian Research Grants Committee -
Grant No. A68/16801.

CONTENTS

Introduction

INTRODUCTION

This book is intended for the student beginning the study of sociolinguistics either at a university or at a tertiary college.   The common complaint has been that often, when starting a new subject, students are overwhelmed by massive reading lists and strings of unfamiliar and unexplained terminology and concepts.   We have attempted to avoid this, moving slowly and, we hope, logically from the micro-level of investigation, e.g. the speech situation, to the discussion of topics which would demand micro- and macro-level (i.e. small and large scope) investigation, e.g. bilingualism and language planning, explaining terms and different approaches as we went along.

It may be objected that we have at times quoted too frequently, giving the writer's name and reference.   This was done deliberately, as a study of a particular topic should not deal only with the subject matter;   one also needs to be familiar with the names of some of the important scholars in the field and the type of research they have done.   A suitable balance is provided by contrasting different approaches to the same topic and by suggesting in *points for discussion* that students should take a critical view of what has been said and enlarge its scope by their own contributions.   The exercises and assignments at the end of each chapter have been designed with the same purpose in mind and the reading list suggested for each topic has been kept deliberately small.

The principal aim of this book is to encourage the development of competency in a fascinating field of study by active participation in its research, even if only in a small way.

A final word of caution and also one of apology.
A book of this type aims at giving what the writers consider the essentials of sociolinguistics and deals briefly with main streams, directions and investigations.   It is obvious that every individual has different views on what is and is not essential.   Therefore some points may have been left out which other writers would have included, and some books and articles omitted - but we rely on the competent lecturer or seminar leader to fill in what he or she considers to be gaps. We feel that we have provided sufficient material to start the ball rolling.

Melbourne   1975   H.K.P. and J.T.P.

CHAPTER 1

1. BEYOND SYNTAX AND SEMANTAX : THE SPEECH SITUATION

1.0   It is not easy to determine *when* sociolinguistics
actually started.   One could agree with Halliday (1973) that
"the linguist's interests have always extended to language as
social behaviour", particularly, when one thinks of such
linguists as J. R. Firth who introduced the term 'sociological
linguistics' in 1935 and the important work of K. L. Pike
(1954-1960) *Language in Relation to a Unified Theory of the
Structure of Human Behavior.*

On the other hand, it has to be admitted that there has
been a considerable shift in emphasis in linguistic research
from phonology and morphology to syntax and semantics and from
there to an increased interest in the study of language in
social context.

When Firth's and Pike's works appeared, many American
linguists, for instance those often referred to as the
Structuralists, were mainly interested in the investigation of
phonology and morphology.   With the development of Generative
Transformational Grammar (Chomsky 1957) there has been an
increasing interest in syntactic problems and later on in
semantics, particularly in the works of a group of linguists
often referred to as Generative Semanticists who are interested
in showing the semantic base structures that underlie syntactic
'surface' structures.   The close interrelationship shown by
some linguists as existing between syntax and semantics has
resulted in the introduction of the term 'semantax'.

For some time, sociologists, anthropologists and social
psychologists have been interested in speech as an indicator
of certain social and/or psychological factors.   In the last
decade, however, more and more linguists have realized that
viewing utterances entirely in isolation is inadequate and that
utterances need to be seen and discussed in relation to the
context in which they occur.

Often, the speaker's presuppositions when making an
utterance are of great importance for a complete understanding
of the semantic concept conveyed.   These presuppositions are
based partially on the speaker's beliefs, attitudes, and the

evaluation of his own role in society and the role of his addressee.

The person to whom the utterance is addressed needs to be considered as well. His reply will show whether or not the speaker's intentions have been achieved or whether the speaker has misjudged factors concerning the listener. Location and time are also of importance. An utterance may be perfectly appropriate on the tennis court but not in a church. Again, it may be appropriate in a church but not during the actual church service.

These and other factors are considered in the analysis of *speech situations*.

1.1   When surveying the emerging interest in aspects of the speech situation, we can distinguish three approaches which are somewhat different in their origin.

(a)   Approach to speech-situational factors by some of the generative semanticists and those who share with them a 'Semantics-Prior' attitude.

(b)   The 'Pragmatic' approach of Dieter Wunderlich and others in Germany.

(c)   The 'Communicative Competence' approach of the American anthropologist Dell Hymes and linguists working along similar lines.

The first two, which are linguistically and philosophically orientated, are by no means unrelated whereas the third more ethnographically orientated approach developed somewhat independently at first.

It must be stressed, of course, that labels are often misleading as they are usually far too definite and that divisions into schools or movements should be seen only as rough guidelines. There are a number of semanticists and sociolinguists interested in problems of the speech situation who take their inspiration from all three approaches.

In this chapter, we shall discuss only the approaches mentioned under (a) and (b) and shall deal with (c) in the next chapter.

1.2   *Austin and Searle*

Both the generative semanticists and the pragmalinguists have been influenced by the writings of the philosophers

J. L. Austin and J. R. Searle.

Austin (1962) when discussing "in which way and which
sense we are using an utterance, e.g. "asking, assuring,
warning, announcing a verdict or intention" introduced the
concept of *illocutionary act.*   Searle has developed this
concept, giving a whole table of Types of Illocutionary Acts
(Request, Assert, Question).

He discusses (1969) the *illocutionary force indicator*
which shows "what illocutionary force the utterance is to have;
that is what illocutionary act the speaker is performing in
the utterance of the sentence.   Illocutionary force indicating
devices in English include at least: word order, stress,
intonation contour, punctuation, the mood of the verb, and the
so-called performative verbs" (e.g. I apologize, I warn, I
state, I promise).   Rules are given for the use of the
illocutionary force indicator (e.g. Pr for Promise) which
operate only if certain conditions are fulfilled, e.g.

> Rule 4 (the sincerity rule)
> "Pr is to be uttered only if S(speaker)
> intends to do A..........."

> Rule 5 (the essential rule)
> "The utterance of Pr counts as the undertaking
> of an obligation to do A..........."

1.3   (a)   *The Generative Semanticists*

It is not proposed here to discuss the work of this
important group of linguists in detail, but in quite a number
of their writings, factors such as speaker's attitudes (often
in the form of presuppositions), time factors (in the form of
quantifier range) and speaker-listener relationship (conversational postulates) which can be termed *speech situational*
have formed an integral part of their arguments.   To quote
just a few examples:

(1)   A fact that has interested generative semanticists for
some time is the problem of presuppositions, i.e. the speaker
makes certain assumptions concerning the listener, or the
situation in general, e.g.

The mâyor is a Republican and the used câr dealer

is honest tóo

requires the presupposition

$(x)(g(x) \supset f(x))$ -   all Republicans are honest

(Green, 1968, G. Lakoff 1971)

R. Lakoff (1971) states in reference to

John is a Republican, but you can trust Bill

"The acceptibility of this sentence does not stem from
necessarily inherent properties of Republicans, but rather from
the speaker's feelings about Republicans, based on personal
prejudice."

(2)   The time factor of the utterance is explored by McCawley
(1971) in 'Tense and time reference in English' when discussing
the range of quantifiers.

'My mother has changed my diapers many times' would be an
appropriate statement for "a precocious 2-year old who still
wore diapers but not for a man who stopped wearing them 30
years ago" - as the present perfect can be used in English only
if the range includes the present tense.

(3)   Dik (1975)   introduces the concept of the evaluative
judgement by the speaker when discussing the difference between
sentence and manner adverbials, e.g. in the case of *wisely*

    John didn't answer the question wisely
                  (Manner Adverbial)

           and

    Wisely, John didn't answer the question
                  (Sentence Adverbial)

In the *sentence adverbial*

Speaker judges that it be $\underline{F}$ of controlling subject X
   to choose/decide (not) to do Y

whereas in the *manner adverbial*

Controlling subject $\underline{X}$ do $\underline{Y}$ in a $\underline{G}$ manner

J. Platt (1973) in his discussion of Sentence Adverbials,
raises the question of '*who* is alleging' in:

Allegedly, Joe embezzled the funds

It is certainly not the speaker or the listener, or, for that
matter, Joe.   The semantic concept of *allegedly* is that the
speaker disclaims responsibility for the assertion he makes.

(4)   An attempt is made by Gordon and Lakoff in their article
'Conversational Postulates' (1971) to "outline a way in which
conversational principles can begin to be formalized and in-
corporated into the theory of generative semantics".   Dealing

with the problem that in many cases a certain utterance can
imply something quite beyond or different from its primary or
literal meaning, they state that given a certain class of contexts CON$_i$ (e.g. boss speaking to employee) and given certain
conversational postulates, 'It's cold in here' (the primary or
literal meaning) entails 'open the window' (the conversationally
implied or conveyed meaning).   We presume this is to let the
hot air in!

POINTS FOR DISCUSSION

The problems raised under (1) - (3) could be
discussed independently of the texts mentioned.
For an understanding of the texts, a knowledge of
some of the principles and methods of Generative
Semantics is necessary.

(1) Look up the first example under (a) and
     discuss whether in fact the presupposition
     stated by Lakoff is correct.   Does the
     speaker *really* wish to imply that *all*
     Republicans are honest or only *some* or *most*?
     How would the speaker defend himself if,
     after his statement, he were challenged by
     the listener?

     What about the *but* example stated by
     Lakoff (1971:67)

     John is a Republican, but he is honest

     Does the speaker wish to imply that *all*
     Republicans are dishonest?

(2) Gordon and Lakoff (1971:65) when discussing
     some conversational postulates, state that
     the following utterances do *not* convey a
     request from the speaker to the hearer to take
     out the garbage:

     (a) I suppose you're going to take out
          the garbage.

     (b) Must you take out the garbage?

     (c) Are you likely to take out the
          garbage?

     (d) Ought you to take out the garbage?

     Can you think of situations where *some* of these
     utterances *could* convey the request to take out

the garbage?   If so, how do they fit into
Gordon and Lakoff's scheme of 'Conversational
Postulates'?   (Read section A and suggest
possibilities)

(3) When dealing with the role of conversational
postulates in a grammar, Gordon and Lakoff
discuss the ambiguity of certain wh-questions,

e.g. 'Why are you painting your house
purple?'

Discuss the ambiguity in the question.
What possible answers could someone give to
such a question?   Why did the speaker not
say: "Unless you have a good reason for
painting your house purple, you shouldn't
paint your house purple."

Check up how Gordon and Lakoff have dealt
with the problem.

1.4 (b) *Pragmalinguistics*

In 1970, Dieter Wunderlich published an article in the
German periodical *Deutschunterricht* on the role of pragmatics
in linguistics (Die Rolle der Pragmatik in der Linguistik)
(1970) in which he discusses the three essential aspects one
has to consider when investigating utterances used in human
communication:

(1) the syntactic aspect

(2) the semantic aspect   and

(3) the pragmatic aspect (seen in relation to
the persons who use the utterances and the
situational and socio-cultural contexts
involved)

In his article 'Sprechakte' (speech acts) (1972a)
Wunderlich sees the writings of the philosopher Charles Sanders
Peirce and of the social psychologist George Herbert Mead as
important bases for his type of pragmatics.   It is one of
Peirce's pragmatic maxims that our concept of an object is the
concept of its effects or, to be more definite, of the effects
which could have practical relevance.

Referring to the speech act theories of Austin and Searle,
Wunderlich develops his interpretation of the speech act.   He

sees communication not only as an exchange of intentions and of
speech content but above all as the establishment of two-way
relations; these then determine a certain level of understanding from which intentions and content get their practical
meaning in the situational context.

Referring to Austin's three kinds of *happiness condition*
(i.e. valid presuppositions, the sincerity condition and the
acceptance by the speaker of certain obligations arising from
the speech act), Wunderlich states that a pragmatics of speech
acts must stipulate which conditions must prevail in order to
cause a certain speech act to be accepted or, in other words,
to be successful. It is not only necessary for the speaker to
make certain assumptions about the hearer (and the general
situation) but in order for a speech act to be successful these
assumptions must also be valid. It would, for instance, be
utterly useless to say to a totally paralysed person "Please
shut the door" or to make that request to anyone if the door is
already shut. One can make one's assumptions in good faith
but they could still be invalid. For instance, one could ask
someone the way to the nearest post office but the person
might be unable to give directions as he himself is a stranger
to the district.

Apart from a variety of articles on the theory of pragmalinguistics, e.g. Maas 'Grammatik und Handlungstheorie'(1972)
there have been a number of analyses and applications, e.g.
Ehlich and Rehbein (1972) deal with speech situations in a
restaurant, Rehbein (1972), dealing with accusations and
excuses, shows in a complex diagram the different phases in a
speech event and the sequencing and interaction of speech acts,
and Flader (1972) investigates the pragmatic aspects of
advertising slogans.

POINTS FOR DISCUSSION

(1) A number of linguists seem to have accepted
     the theories expressed by Austin and Searle
     about speech acts. Was this a good develop-
     ment or did it divorce their investigations
     of speech acts too much from reality?

(2) Does Pragmalinguistics seem too concerned
     with the *effects* that a speech act achieves?

(3) In certain contexts, an utterance can
     function as two or more different speech
     acts, e.g.

(i)   A student is asked by his mother:

"Shouldn't you be off now?"

Is she asking him a question or
telling him it's time to go, or is
she requesting him to get out of
the house because he is irritating
her?   Or is there a situation where
all three are intended?

(ii) Little Mary is playing naked in the
garden on a very hot day.   A
neighbour says to Mary's mother:

"Should little Mary be left like that?"

Is she simply asking a question to get
information from the mother, i.e. is
she indirectly asking whether Mary's
mother is aware of the state of affairs
(danger to Mary's health, etc.) or is
she making a request or suggestion to
Mary's mother, namely "do something
about it!", or is she stating that she
is horrified by the unfeeling mother
and/or the indecent exposure of three
year old Mary?   Or are all three
functions involved to a greater or
lesser extent?

Try to think of other examples where utterances
can have more than one function in a certain situation.

(4)   An utterance could have different functions if
the speaker intended it (a) for the obvious
addressee and (b) for another person (or other
persons) who are also present but not directly
addressed, e.g.

(i)   At a party, A is turning to B and
says in the hearing of the hostess:
"This sponge cake is delicious."
She wishes to make

(a)   a statement that flatters
the hostess   and
(b)   a suggestion to B to have
some of the cake

(ii) The barman is shouting to a burly
attendant whilst pointing to an

unwanted customer:
"I don't think this guy wants to
stay here much longer!"
This utterance would have the double
function of a request (get rid of
him) and a warning to the customer
(if you don't clear out at once you'll
get chucked out).

Can you think of similar instances of double
function for utterances in certain situations?

EXERCISES (a)

(1)   What are the speaker's presuppositions
regarding the listener in the following
statements:

(a)   You like strong drink, don't
you?   Would you like a beer?

(b)   This music is by Beethoven but
it's not hard to listen to.

Give alternative interpretations in each
case of the speaker's own attitudes to
strong drink, beer and Beethoven.

(2)   (i)   Show the distinction between the
following sentences:

(a) He answered the question foolishly.

(b) Foolishly, he answered the
question.

(ii) State *who* is *supposing* or *alleging* in
the following sentences:
Is it the speaker?

(a) Supposedly, Joe's coming.

(b) Allegedly, Joe embezzled the funds.

(3)   What is the *sincerity condition* pertaining to

Go downstairs to the kitchen and fetch me
the red book on the kitchen table.

said by a mother to her little girl.   She
wishes the child out of the way so that she

can tell a dirty joke to her girl friend.
She knows that there is no red book on the
kitchen table.   Is there any *sincerity*
involved in her request?

EXERCISES (b)

(1)   (i) The window is open and you wish
            someone to shut it for you.   Give
            as many utterances as you can think
            of which could convey this request
            to someone and describe briefly the
            situation in which you would use it
            and your relationship to the listener.

      (ii) Would you consider the following
            utterances suitable for the purpose
            stated in (i)?   Why?   Why not?

           (a) I really have to get a
               cardigan.

           (b) You know, I really feel at
               my best when the temperature
               is in the high thirties
               (Celsius).

           (c) Do you want me to put a
               paperweight on these docu-
               ments?   They seem to be
               blowing about a lot!

(2)   Give a number of different contexts in
      which the following utterance would have
      different functions (e.g. function as a
      question, a request etc. - if different
      intonation is used)

          You are coming this evening

(3)   When would the presuppositions contained in
      the following statements be *false*?

      (i)   Betty's youngest child has the
            measles.

      (ii) Fred's mother-in-law is coming
            to stay with him.

      (iii) The Millers have sold their new
            house.

(iv)   I'd like to have my pencil back,
       please.

(v)   Stop beating your wife!

ASSIGNMENT

Wunderlich states that "in a given situation,
entirely different utterances can have one and the
same function".   Would these be the same types of
utterance in every language?   Take the English
utterances you have found in Exercise (b)(1)(i) or
make up new English examples in a new situation.
Then compare these with the utterances you would
use in the same context in another language (or
other languages).   In what way do they differ from
the first set?

RECOMMENDED   READING

(a) and (b)

Austin   J. L. (1962) 1971.   *How to do things with words.*
          London : Oxford University Press.

          A stimulating book which does not presuppose a great
          deal of philosophical training.

Searle   J. R. 1969.   *Speech acts.   An essay in the
          philosophy of language.*   London : Cambridge
          University Press.

          A detailed discussion of various aspects of the
          speech act.   Presupposes a certain knowledge of
          symbolic logic.   Chapter 3 'The structure of
          illocutionary acts' is probably the most important
          section of the book.

          (1965) 1972.   What is a speech act?   In *Language
          and social context,* ed. P.P. Giglioli, pp 136-154.
          Harmondsworth : Penguin.

          This article was first published in 1965 in
          Philosophy in America, M. Black ed., pp 221-39.
          It deals in a slightly less complex way with some
          of the points discussed in Chapter 3 of Speech acts
          mentioned above, although the latter is less dis-
          jointed than the article and is recommended for
          preference.

(a)

Gordon   D. and Lakoff, G. 1971.   Conversational postulates.
In Papers from the Seventh Regional Meeting, Chicago
Linguistic Society.

A very interesting, stimulating article but requires
a knowledge of predicate calculus or some of the
principle methods of the generative semanticists.

Fillmore   C. and Langendoen D. T. eds. 1971.   *Studies in
linguistic semantics.*   New York : Holt, Rinehart
& Winston.

A collection of articles on semantics, some
incorporating points on certain speech situational
factors:
       e.g. Lakoff, G. pp. 62-70
Some knowledge of predicate calculus will be useful.

(b)

The books mentioned here have not, to the writers' knowledge,
appeared in an English translation.

Maas U. and Wunderlich, D.   1972.   *Pragmatik und sprachliches
Handeln.*   Frankfurt : Athenäum Verlag.

Wunderlich D. ed. 1972.   *Linguistische Pragmatik.*
Frankfurt : Athenäum Verlag.

CHAPTER 2

2. ASPECTS OF COMMUNICATIVE COMPETENCE

2.0   In 1962, Dell Hymes conceived of a new area of study
which he felt had been neglected up to then.   He called it
the *ethnography of speaking*.   He saw it as filling a gap
between what is usually described in grammars and what is
usually described in ethnographies (*1).   In other words
(Hymes 1962) "it is a question of what a child internalizes
about speaking, beyond the rules of grammar and a dictionary,
while becoming a full-fledged member of its speech community.
Or, it is a question of what a foreigner must learn about a
group's verbal behavior in order to participate appropriately
and effectively in its activities.   The ethnography of speaking is concerned with the situations and uses, the patterns and
functions of speaking as an activity in its own right".

     In later publications (1964, 1972, 1974), Hymes somewhat
widens the scope of his original concept and changes its name
to *ethnography of communication*.   He stresses (1964) that
"not language but communication must provide the frame of
reference within which the place of language in culture and
society is to be described".

     Hymes' views of language as an essential part of social
communication made him naturally critical (1972a) of Chomsky's
concepts of competence and performance (*2) and Chomsky's maxim
that "linguistic theory is concerned primarily with an ideal
speaker-listener, in a completely homogeneous speech community"
(Chomsky 1965).   Acquisition of the Chomsky-type of competence
in a certain language would not take into account essential
socio-cultural features, so important for communication.   Even
Chomsky's theory of performance, although it is equated with a
theory of language use, is not basically concerned with social
interactions.

     A child possessing a Chomsky-type competence would produce
and understand all the grammatical sentences of a language but
would not have acquired the knowledge of how and when to use
them and to whom.   In other words, the child would not only
produce any sentence at random but would also produce speech
and silence at random.   Such a child, says Hymes (1972a) would
"be likely to be institutionalized", and he goes on to say that

"We have to account for the fact that a normal child acquires knowledge of sentences, not only as grammatical, but also as appropriate. He or she acquires competence as to when to speak, when not, and as to what to talk about with whom, when, where and in what manner. In short, a child becomes able to accomplish a repertoire of speech acts, to take part in speech events and to evaluate their accomplishment by others". Thus he advocates a wider concept of competence which includes the factors mentioned above and which he terms *communicative competence*.

DISCUSSION

If you are familiar with Chomsky's book *Aspects of the Theory of Syntax* (1965) or if you are interested in his views on performance (1965, chapter 1, particularly 1-5 and 30-37) discuss whether or not Hymes' interpretation of Chomsky's definition of performance is correct. You may also like to consult Katz (1967).

2.1   *Speech Situations, Speech Events and Speech Acts*

The speech situation.   There are many situations which are associated with speech, e.g. ceremonies, meals, sports matches. Apart from non-verbal events they may contain a number of speech events which need not necessarily be of the same type.

Hymes (1972b) states that a *speech event* "is restricted to activities or aspects of activities that are directly governed by rules or norms for the use of speech".

A speech event could be clearly demarcated, e.g. a lecture, a formal speech, a prayer in which the minister and the congregation alternate. Rather more vaguely demarcated speech events would be conversations and discussions. Speech events usually consist of several speech acts but they may contain just one,

> e.g. a shout to the bystanders "Help!"
> before the fatal shot is fired.

To summarize:

(1)   A barbecue in the garden would be a *speech situation*

(2)   A conversation at the barbecue between Jack and Jill would be a *speech event,* and

(3)   The question by Jack to Jill (during the
      conversation):   "Would you like to meet my
      parents at the weekend?" would be a *speech act*.
      Jill's answer to Jack's question would be a
      further speech act.

If there are more than one speech act in the speech event,
the correct sequencing of the speech acts is often of great
importance for the purpose of communication.   This factor will
be discussed in more detail later on.

The *speech act* "represents a level distinct from the
sentence" and "is not identifiable with any single portion of
other levels of grammar" (Hymes 1972b).

DISCUSSION

Hymes' attitude to the attempts of the
generative semanticists to include speech act
phenomena in their theory can be seen from the
following statement:

> "Some linguists, recognizing the signifi-
> cance of speech acts, now wish to incor-
> porate them into syntax, so that a sentence
> carries with it in the deep structure a
> performative verb, something like 'I ask
> you', 'I tell you' and the like (normally
> deleted in overt form).   There is indeed
> evidence to support this approach in
> some cases (McCawley 1968:157) but as a
> general solution to the problem it is
> cumbersome and counterintuitive, and
> appears a last-ditch effort to keep
> within the conventional boundaries of
> linguistics.   An approach that insists
> on the complex abstract knowledge of
> speakers with regard to other relation-
> ships quite distinct from manifest
> forms need not cling to literal verbal
> embodiment of acts of speech......
> Some assertions, requests, commands,
> threats, and the like are known to be
> such on the basis of a knowledge *jointly*
> of the message form and the relation-
> ship in which it occurs."

Discuss whether or not you find Hymes' arguments
convincing.   You may also like to look at the article

by McCawley (1968) 'The role of semantics in a
grammar' to which Hymes refers in this excerpt.

2.2   The Components of a Speech Act

Over the past years, Hymes has somewhat changed and
elaborated on his definitions of the components of a speech
act.   In later publications, he has added several new concepts
(Hymes 1972b, 1974).   We shall therefore not refer to individual publications but acknowledge our general indebtedness to
Hymes in the following discussions as regards terminology and
certain definitions.   Most explications and all examples and
exercises are our own.

(a)   *The Participants*

One can distinguish between 4 types of participants

(i)   The Speaker or Sender

(ii)   The Addressor

(iii)   The Hearer, Listener, Receiver or Audience

(iv)   The Addressee

It is not possible to claim that (i) and (ii) on the one
hand, and (iii) and (iv) on the other hand are necessarily
the same.

In some situations we would find both a sender and an
addressor, e.g. in most TV commercials (sender = firm advertising the product, addressor = actor or announcer delivering the
message), in a domestic situation (mother = sender, elder
brother = addressor, younger brother playing at a neighbour's
house = hearer/addressee of mother's message).

In other situations, there would be a hearer (audience)
and an addressee, e.g. a prize giving ceremony at a school
(prize winners = addressees (*3) the fond relatives = audience),
in a domestic scene (sender/addressor = father, addressee (*3)
= mother, audience = children).   The participants who feature
as 'receiver or audience' in such a combination may be just as
significant as the addressee.   They could be indirectly
addressed, e.g. warned, requested to do something, etc.   It
would be significant whether in certain social groups those
present would be considered as audience by the speaker or
whether their presence would just be ignored, e.g. children and
servants.

In some communities, spirits, plants and stones (the
latter often as representatives of spirits) may feature as
addressees.   Even in Westernized so-called 'advanced'
societies, it is common to consider pets as addressees and to
anthropomorphise them, attributing to them the ability to
respond.   Pets can, of course, feature conveniently as
addressees in a 3-participant event when for instance the wife
tells her lap dog (with her husband as 'audience')

    Oh, you poor little diddums - that nasty master
        of yours should have given you your bickies
        long ago.

Hymes does not specify any particular hierarchy concerning
his participant terms.   However, we see sender/speaker and
receiver/hearer as more primary concepts as, after all, they
are the 'originator' of the message and the one for whom it is
intended.   Addressor and addressee, *if separated from the
above* are after all only the 'deliverer' and the 'sounding
board' of the message.   Therefore, we would like to consider
that, by a redundancy rule, the speaker/sender is also the
addressor and the hearer/receiver the addressee unless otherwise stated.

Another somewhat confusing array is created by 'speaker/
sender' on the one hand and 'hearer, listener, receiver,
audience' on the other.   In many cases it is clear, of course,
which one of the set would be the most suitable term.   However,
apart from the fact that there are many borderline cases, most
of these terms have additional connotations which may obtrude.
To have overall cover terms, we suggest S-Participant for the
originator of the message (i.e. the sender or speaker) and
R-Participant for the one for whom the message is intended
(i.e. the hearer, listener, receiver or the audience).

An important factor in the communication between S- and
R- Participants is their role relationship.   In some speech
events, roles are fixed by the social status both participants
hold in the community (e.g. the speaker may be a judge, government minister or important business man - the hearer may be a
person of lower social status, or vice versa).   Or the two
participants could hold positions of a different status in an
employment situation (e.g. director-secretary, accountant-
typist).   However, there are also the indefinable indirect
roles that people assume in every day conversation.

Even among friends it is rare for the role relationship
between them to be entirely even.   If none of them is perman-
ently in a dominant position, usually one of the participants

tries to take temporary ascendancy over the other one who then
may try to reverse the role relationship again with his next
speech act.   There are many strategies that could be used to
gain 'role ascendancy'.   Here are just a few examples:

A to B (referring to past ascendancy) "I told you........."
                                      "I warned you......."
                                      "I've always said..."

        (pity) "You poor thing........"
               "I really feel for you.."

        (ridicule) "You silly thing.   Really, you can do
                    better than that!"

        (hidden threat) "I really ought to tell Bill about
                         it....."

        (pretending to mediate) "Don't worry, I'll talk to
                                 her and explain everything......."
                                 "Why don't you let me put
                                 in a good word for you.........?"

(b)   *Message Form and Content*

     Both of these components are of great importance in a
speech act.   The form in which a message is transmitted will
facilitate or hinder the successful transmission of the content
of the message.

(c)   *Setting and Scene*

     Hymes makes a difference between the two concepts in the
way that *setting* refers to the time and place of a speech act
and in general to the physical circumstances whereas *scene*
designates the psychological setting or the cultural definition
of a certain type of scene.

     For instance, a church hall (a location belonging to a
setting) could become at certain times the *scene* of a special
celebration, a table-tennis tournament or a local dance.   A
creek bed in a tribal territory in Central Australia could, in
its dry state, be the *scene* of a secret ceremony by the tribal
women and, in its wet state, a playground for the children of
the tribe.

(d)   *Channel*

The type of channel could be oral, written, telegraphic, etc.
Aboriginal tribes of Australia used elaborate smoke signals to
convey their messages whereas some African tribes used drum

beats.   Oral channels could vary according to whether there is
an actual physical presence of the S- and R- Participants (e.g.
'face to face' speech events) or a distance between them (e.g.
telephone conversations) as this would have a bearing on the
Message Form and Content.

(e)   *Forms of Speech*

Hymes mentions a number of concepts such as languages,
dialects, codes, varieties, registers and styles.   Some of
these will be discussed in more detail in the next two chapters.

When one considers aspects such as the common origin of a
lexicon and grammatical structures it seems more appropriate to
Hymes to speak of *languages* and *dialects*.   However, when considering mutual intelligibility he suggests the term *code*.

(f)   Hymes introduces 3 further components (i) *Purpose-
outcomes,* the conventionally recognized and expected outcomes
of a speech event.   (ii) *Purpose-goals,* the goals that the
participants wish to achieve and (iii) *Key,* the tone, manner or
spirit in which the act is done, e.g. mock, serious, perfunct-
ory, etc.   The signalling of a key may be by verbal or non-
verbal means (a wink, gestures, postures, musical accompaniment).

Obviously, there is a close inter-relationship between the
components which must be realized when focussing on one or
other of them in a discussion.

POINTS   FOR   DISCUSSION

(1)   In what way could the message form or content
        be distorted if the participants in a speech
        act were

        (a) the sender   (b) the addressor and
        (c) the R- participant   e.g. a mother
        sending a child with a message to her
        neighbour.

(2)   Is it true that there is a definite change in
        role relationships in conversation between
        friends?   Or is one of them always the
        dominant participant?   Think of some conversa-
        tions you have had with your friends recently
        and try to analyse them.

(3)   Message form and content are involved in
        relation to the appropriate length of the

message.

What is wrong with B's response?

A. Morning, Sam.   Lovely morning, isn't
    it?

B. Well, I don't quite agree with you
    Basil.   The humidity has increased
    rather much in the last two hours.
    In fact it's now 74% and with a
    temperature of 24°C I find this a
    little oppressive.   Nothing like as
    bad as Darwin in the rainy season,
    of course, but not quite ideal.

Can you think of other examples of responses
that are inappropriate mainly because of
their length (either too short or too long)?

2.3   *Rules governing the Use of Speech*

Susan Ervin-Tripp (1969, 1972) gives three important
types of rules governing verbal output in a social setting:

(a) Alternation Rules   (b) Co-occurrence Rules and
(c) Sequencing Rules.

The first type, *alternation rules,* concerns the choice
among alternative ways of speaking.   Her example is the
American Rules of Address.   In a complex but clearly set out
diagram (shown on page 21) which is to be read like a computer
flow chart she shows the various alternatives of address which
are open to a "competent adult member of a Western American
academic community" (1972).   She stresses, however, that the
sequences shown in the diagram may not necessarily show the
actual sequence of decisions made by the individual speaker
when choosing the appropriate form of address.

The diagram is entered at the point of the arrow.   The
diamonds indicate selectors.   By following either the + or -
path indication of the selectors, various final choices can be
made.

Status marked situations refer to courtrooms and formal
meetings, where status is clearly specified.

Rank refers to a hierarchy within a working group, or to
ranked statuses like teacher-pupil.

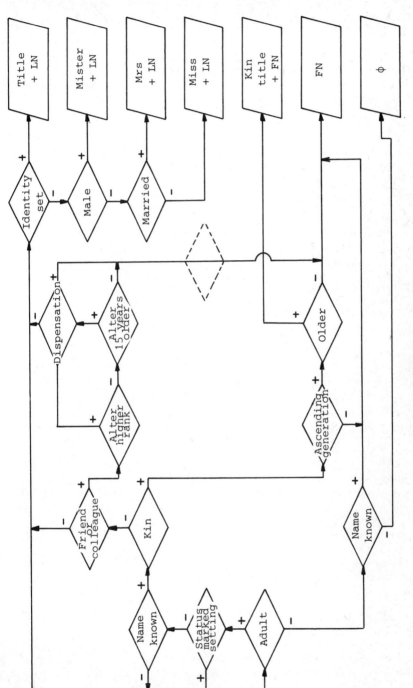

Fig. 1. An American address system.

Identity Set refers to a list of occupational titles or
courtesy titles e.g. Judge, Doctor, Professor.

One of the basic sociolinguistic studies on forms of
address is the work of Brown and Gilman (1960) on the informal
and formal singular pronouns of address in many European
languages.   In English, two pronouns 'thou-you' existed but
'thou' is no longer used except in some religious contexts.
In Russian, the contrast is realized by *ty* and *vy*, in German by
du and *Sie* and in French by *tu* and *vous*.   The two pronouns
(T-V) are seen as closely associated with "two dimensions funda-
mental to the analysis of all social life - the dimensions of
power and solidarity".   Investigating what they term 'the
power semantic' and the 'solidarity semantic', Brown and Gilman
claim that there was an abstract conflict between the two in
certain areas and that it is in the process of being resolved
in the direction of solidarity.

Below are some examples of social dyads involving
(a) semantic conflict and (b) their resolution.

Friedrich has done some interesting work on the social
significance of pronominal usage in Russian (1964, 1966, 1972).
Among the ten features he considers of importance in accounting
for Russian pronominal usage are: social context (setting,
scene), characteristics of participants, i.e. age, generation,
sex, genealogical distance, relative authority, group membership (1972).   Ervin-Tripp (1972) devised a diagram of the 19th
century Russian address system based on information supplied in
Friedrich which is shown on page 23.

Special status refers to the tsar and God, *status-marked
settings* refer to court, parliament, duels, etc., *rank
inferiors* might be lower in social class or army rank, or be
servants, *solidarity* applies to classmates, fellow students,
fellow revolutionaries, lovers and intimate friends.

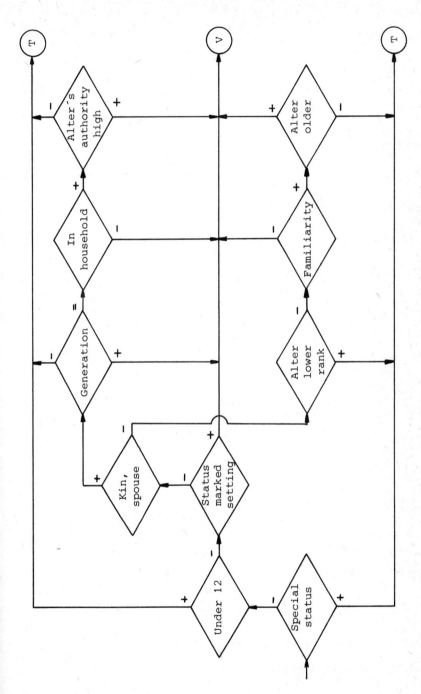

Fig. 2.   Nineteenth century Russian address.

Neustupný (1968) when discussing politeness systems,
considers apart from 'communicativeness' and 'status', such
features as F_3 - intimacy, F_4 - sex, F_6 - instantaneous status
feature (e.g. mastery of situation, personal excellence, thank-
fulness) and F_7 - instantaneous intimacy (e.g. feeling of close-
ness).

F_6 is of particular interest as it relates to the personal
struggle for role ascendancy in speech events which we mentioned
earlier in this chapter.

POINTS FOR DISCUSSION

(1)   Discuss Ervin-Tripp's diagram Fig. 1 on page 21
      and decide to what extent it would fit the
      address system in your speech community.
      Suggest necessary alterations.

(2)   Although the distinctions between 'thou'
      and 'you' can no longer be used in
      English, there are, however, means of
      address or other devices by which the status-
      relation or intimacy-relation between the
      participants of a speech event can be marked.
      Can you think of some?

(3)   Metcalf (1936) when discussing forms of
      address in 18th century Germany, related
      the following:

          "The fact that a journeyman artisan
          accorded a student ER aroused such
          protest at the University of
          Göttingen that a great part of the
          student body left town .... A
          similar incident in Mainz created
          such disorder that the elector was
          forced to call in troops."

      The third person singular form er (he) as a
      form of address was used at the end of the
      18th century mainly to subordinates instead
      of du (informal 'you') and Sie (formal 'you').
      Can you think of other instances where speech
      varieties still use or have used a form of
      address which is equivalent to the 3rd person
      singular? What is/was the status of this
      form in the pronominal address system of the
      speech variety?

(4) Read the article by Brown and Gilman
'The Pronouns of power and solidarity'
(1960) and discuss whether or not you
agree with their ideas on the 'general
semantic evolution' of T and V.

(5) If you have some knowledge of the Russian
address system in the USSR at present,
discuss how it differs from that of 19th
century Russia as shown in the work by
Friedrich (1964, 1966, 1972) and the
diagram of Ervin-Tripp Fig. 2 on page 23.

(b) *Co-occurrence Rules*

Ervin-Tripp (1972) called the rules governing selection
co-occurrence rules. Vertical co-occurrence rules specify the
realization of an item at each of the levels of structure of a
language. For instance, given a syntactical form, only
certain lexicon may normally be employed, and a particular set
of phonetic values may be realized in the lexicon. Violation
of the rules could result in bizarre structures like this one
(quoted by Ervin-Tripp 1972)

"How's it going your Eminence? Centrifuging OK?
Also have you been analysin' watch' unnertook
t'achieve?"

An example from an Australian setting (Platt 1974) would
be if someone at an official function got up and stated:

"On this auspicious occasion, me 'n me cobbers
feel highly privileged to 'ave the chance to talk
ter youze jokers."

DISCUSSION

If you are familiar with American and/or
Australian speech try to analyse which co-
occurrence rules have not been observed in the
two examples quoted above.

(c) *Sequencing Rules*

As mentioned earlier, there are certain rules relating
to the appropriate sequence of speech acts in a speech event.
In some speech events, e.g. an exchange of speech within a
ritual, the sequencing would be very strictly adhered to.
There are, however, many instances in daily life, e.g. in a

telephone conversation, greetings, leave taking etc., where a definite type of sequencing has to be followed.

Ervin-Tripp (1969) analyses an event of leave taking (LT) between two participants. She sees it as consisting of two parts

LT 1 + LT 2

LT 1 ──────────> Goodbye + CP

CP ──────────> $\left\{\begin{array}{l}\text{I am very glad to have met you}\\\text{I hope I shall see you again}\end{array}\right.$ $\left\{\begin{array}{l}\text{soon}\\\text{sometime}\end{array}\right\}$

LT 2 ──────────> Thank you (I hope so, too)

Taking telephone conversations as our next example, the answerer speaks first whether it is just "hullo" or "Brown's the florist" or the announcement of the telephone number, say "323-7516". The caller would then be obliged to speak, usually giving his identification and/or requesting a third person to be fetched to the phone.

That certain utterances take on special functions in a speech event such as a telephone conversation can be seen from the following sequence:

A (male voice):   Hullo

B: Hullo, this is Pete Smith, is
                   Mary at home?

(1) *inappropriate* A: Yes (puts down receiver)

(2) *appropriate* A: Yes - just hold on a minute, I'll
                   get her.

(3) *appropriate* A: No - sorry. She's not at home
                   at the moment. (Shall I
                   get her to call you when she
                   gets back?)

The reason for the inappropriateness of reply (1) is that B's speech act did not have the function of a straightforward yes-no question but it was really a request signifying: 'If Mary *is* at home, I would like to speak to her.'

If A (maybe an irate father) did not wish to agree to this request he could have appropriately replied:

Yes, Mary is at home but I won't allow you to talk to

her   or (more authoritarian)

Mary is not at home *for you*!

Some interesting investigations on correct and incorrect sequencing have been done by Schegloff (1972) and Sacks, Schegloff and Jefferson (1974).

DISCUSSION

Would it be possible to grade speech events according to the degree of rigidity required in sequencing the speech acts within them?   Are there speech events which allow for no optional sequence?   Are there some where sequencing is unnecessary?

EXERCISES

(1)   It has been mentioned that a speech event can consist of just one single speech act, e.g. "Murder!", "Help!", "Fire!" shouted to passers-by. Give more examples and briefly describe the situation for each.

(2)   Give some examples of

(i)   the same speech act being a part of different speech events,

and

(ii)   the same speech event being a part of different speech situations.

(3)   Give several examples where one *setting* can serve as different *scenes*.

(4)   Ervin-Tripp (1972:223) mentions the following real speech event where the participants were a negro physician and a policeman:

'What's your name, boy?'

'Dr. Poussaint, I'm a physician.'

'What's your first name, boy?'

'Alvin'

and she states "The policeman insulted Dr.

Poussaint three times". Explain the
insults in terms of the American address
system (Fig. 1) on page 21. Can you
think of similar instances?

(5) Using Ervin-Tripp's diagram of the American
address system on page 21 as a guide, draw
a diagram representing the address system
used in your speech variety.

(6) Your own speech variety may have a pronominal
T-V distinction or an even more complex one.
On the other hand, you may be familiar with
a speech variety where such distinctions
are used. Show this pronominal usage by
drawing a type of diagram similar to the one
used by Ervin-Tripp in relation to 19th
century Russian.

(7) Collect closing sequences of various speech
events and comment on the way they differ,
taking into account information about all
the participants, topic, setting, scene etc.

ASSIGNMENTS

(1) Give a detailed analysis of a brief speech
event between two participants, taking into
account all the points that have been discussed in this chapter.

(2) You may be familiar with the works of one
author or of several authors which are all
set in a particular speech community at a
particular time in history. Make an
analysis of the T-V usage as shown in these
works. You may like to use Friedrich (1972)
as a guide for this exercise. One word of
warning: Make sure the authors are reliable
in depicting the pronominal usage of the time.
Consulting grammars, letters and autobiograph-
ies of the period might be an advisable way of
checking.

(3) Make an investigation of the pet-owners among
your friends/relations/neighbours. Do they
treat their pet as an R- participant + addressee

(e.g. capable of understanding all their
messages) or just use it in speech acts
as an addressee when indirectly addressing
a third person (the R- participant) or both?
Make a table of your findings. Do they vary
with the type of pet, the speaker's attitude
to animals/birds or the social status, age or
sex of the speaker?

(4) In order to ascertain differences among French,
German and Italian in the usage of T and V,
Brown and Gilman (1960) administered questionnaires to native speakers of the three languages
in the form of:

1.(a) Which pronoun would you use in speaking
to your mother?

T (definitely) -
T (probably)   -
Possibly T, possibly V -
V (probably) -
V (definitely) -

1.(b) Which would she use in speaking to you?

T (definitely) -
T (probably)   -
Possibly T, possibly V -
V (probably) -
V (definitely) -

If you know some native speakers of two or more
languages which still use the T-V distinction,
try to administer similar tests to them.

Brown and Gilman suggest asking questions
about usage between the subject and his mother,
father, grandfather, wife, younger brother or
sister who are still children, a married elder
brother, brother's wife, remote male cousin,
elderly female servant, fellow students,former
school friends. Questions are also asked about
T-V usage between employees, employer-employee,
officer-soldier, customer-waiter in a restaurant
etc.

This is quite a comprehensive list to start with,
but you may like to alter it by adding different

participants and omitting some which have been
suggested.

RECOMMENDED READING

Hymes   D. 1972a.   On communicative competence.   In
           Sociolinguistics, J. B. Pride and J. Holmes eds.,
           269-293.   Harmondsworth: Penguin.

           1972b.   Models of the interaction of language and
           social life.   In *Directions in sociolinguistics*,
           J. J. Gumperz and D. Hymes eds., 35 - 71.   New
           York: Holt, Rinehart and Winston.

           1974.   *Foundations in sociolinguistics.   An
           ethnographic approach.*   Philadelphia: University
           of Pennsylvania Press.

           This is a collection of a number of his articles in
           revised form.   It includes some of the material of
           1972a and 1972b.

Ervin-Tripp S.   (1969) 1971.   Sociolinguistics.   In *Advances
           in the sociology of language I,* J. Fishman ed.,
           15-91.   The Hague: Mouton.

           First published in 1969 in *Advances in experimental
           social psychology.*   L. Berkowitz ed., 91-165.
           New York: Academic Press.

           1972.   On sociolinguistic rules: alternation and
           co-occurrence.   In *Directions in sociolinguistics*,
           J. J. Gumperz and D. Hymes eds., 213-250.   New York:
           Holt Rinehart and Winston.

           The two articles contain similar material but are not
           quite identical.

Brown R. and Gilman A. (1960) 1972.   The pronouns of power and
           solidarity.   In *Language and social context,* P. P.
           Giglioli ed., 252-282.   Harmondsworth: Penguin.

           First published in *Style in language,* T. A. Sebeok
           ed., 253-276.   Cambridge, Mass.:   M.I.T. Press.

Footnotes

(*1)   Ethnography is the scientific description of the races
       of man.

(*2)   In Chomsky's view,
       linguistic *competence* is the speaker/hearer's implicit
       knowledge of language structure, enabling him to
       produce and understand an infinite set of sentences in
       his language;   linguistic *performance* is the actual
       use of language in concrete situations.

(*3)   It may be argued that the 'prize winners' and the
       'mother' in the examples are more than just
       'addressees' but that it would be more appropriate
       in these cases to talk of 'primary receiver' and
       'secondary receiver'.   For a more detailed discussion
       of these two concepts, see chapter 10.

3.   THE   SPEECH   COMMUNITY,   REPERTOIRES   AND   DOMAINS

3.1   *The Speech Community*

An important concept in the discussion of communication is the *speech community*.   It is interesting that, when comparing the definitions of that concept over the past decades, a definite shift from purely linguistic to more sociolinguistic criteria can be observed.

Bloomfield (1933) defined the speech community as "a group of people who use the same system of speech signals".   Chomsky (1965) refers to the "completely homogeneous speech community" whose speakers know its language perfectly.

Gumperz made a break with this type of definition (1968) when he contrasted the formal analysis of language with the analysis of linguistic phenomena within a socially defined universe.   The former, he states, has as its object of attention "a particular body of linguistic data ... abstracted from the settings in which it occurs" whereas the latter is a study of "language usage as it reflects more general behavior norms".   The 'socially defined universe' mentioned above he identifies as the *speech community* and gives it the following definition:

"Any human aggregate characterized by means of a shared body of verbal signs and set off from similar aggregates by significant differences in language use."

Most groups of any permanence no matter how small may be treated as speech communities, e.g. nations or smaller sub-regions thereof, occupational associations or even certain gangs.

Hymes (1974) accuses Bloomfield, Chomsky and others of having "reduced the notion of speech community to that of lang-uage by equating the two" and of having thereby made 'speech community' a redundant concept.   Hymes sees the speech community as a social rather than a linguistic entity.   One must start investigations with a social group and must consider

all the linguistic varieties present in it and the way they are
organized.   It would be wrong to make the concept of 'language'
a starting point for investigation - as the concept of
'language' in itself can be an extremely confusing one.   In
region A several speech varieties may be counted as dialects of
the same language, whereas in region B, speech varieties which
are closer to one another linguistically speaking than the
'dialects' in A, may for political reasons be considered as
different languages.

Furthermore, a grammatical knowledge of the forms of
speech alone is not sufficient to make one a member of a
particular speech community, e.g. some scholars might have a
reading knowledge of several languages but not be able to
express themselves appropriately in speech situations in these
languages.   On the other hand a knowledge of the rules of
'speaking' alone is not sufficient either.   Referring to
Neustupný's useful concept of *Sprechbund* (1969) for the
"phenomenon of shared features of speaking across language
boundaries" (e.g. shared norms of greeting, sequencing etc.),
Hymes states that a knowledge of usage patterns alone is not
sufficient either for being considered a member of a certain
speech community.   His definition of a speech community is
then: "A community sharing knowledge of rules for the conduct
and interpretation of speech.   Such sharing comprises knowledge of at least one form of speech, and knowledge also of its
patterns of use.   Both conditions are necessary" (1974).

He does, however, realize that further criteria may be
necessary to cover the notions of 'community' and of membership
of a community in the societal sense.   For the present he has
decided to reserve the notion of community for a local unit,
characterized for its members by common locality and primary
interaction.

                    POINTS   FOR   DISCUSSION

    (1)   Is Hymes correct in his criticism of Bloom-
          field and Chomsky regarding the definition of
          'speech community'?   Or are there various
          aspects from which one can consider 'speech
          community' which are all equally useful?

    (2)   Could the speakers of Esperanto be considered
          a 'speech community' according to the
          definitions given by Gumperz and Hymes?   In
          order to explore this point more fully, it
          is suggested that you read the Gumperz
          article mentioned in the Reading List at the

end of the chapter, as well as Chapter 2
of Hymes (1974).

3.2 *Speech Repertoires*

A member of a speech community need not have communicative
competence in just *one* speech variety.   He could be competent
in quite a number of them.   This claim does not seem so hard
to accept when we consider that speech varieties, after all,
need not mean what is generally interpreted as 'languages',
i.e. certain national languages like French, German, Russian.
A *speech variety* could be a national language but it could also
refer to a geographical or a social dialect (sociolect) or to
specialized varieties (e.g. occupational varieties).   The
comparatively neutral term *speech variety* is a useful one in
sociolinguistic investigations as it does not have the array of
semantic connotations that are often involved in the concept of
'language'.

A *speech repertoire* can thus be tentatively defined as the
range of linguistic varieties which the speaker has at his
disposal.

It may be argued that verbal repertoires can only be
viewed with regard to a speech community of which the speaker
is a member.   In fact, most sociologists and sociolinguists
have considered the term 'repertoire' in relation to certain
speech communities under investigation, e.g. Fishman (1972d)
states that not only multilingual but also monolingual speech
communities utilize a repertoire of language varieties.   In
monolingual speech communities the linguistic network may
consist of several social class, regional and occupational
varieties of the same language.

It may be appropriate, when investigating the speech
varieties in use in certain speech communities, to change the
definition of speech repertoire given above to:

> *A speech repertoire is the range of linguistic*
> *varieties which the speaker has at his disposal and*
> *which he may appropriately use as a member of his*
> *speech community.*

However, in certain cases one may wish to refer to a
speaker's individual verbal repertoire.   For instance, in a
general investigation which has been started by the writers on
the Singapore English speech continuum (Platt 1975a, 1975b), it
was found that, for the younger age group, the domestic lang-

uage backgrounds, i.e. the verbal repertoires (VR's) of their
parents, varied considerably - e.g.

Case A: Father's VR : CSE (Colloquial Singapore English),
                        Mandarin, Native Southern Chinese
                        Dialect I, Bazaar Malay.

          Mother's VR : Native Southern Chinese Dialect I,
                        Bazaar Malay.

Case B: Father's VR : FSE (Formal Singapore English), CSE,
                        Mandarin, Native Southern Chinese
                        Dialect II, Bazaar Malay.

          Mother's VR : FSE, CSE, Malay.

In the field of application of Sociolinguistics to
Education, there are also instances where the individual verbal
repertoire of a speaker must be considered, e.g. in TESL
(Teaching English as a Second Language) to migrant groups of
mixed origin and in TEFL (Teaching English as a Foreign
Language) to Asian students who may be members of the same
wider speech community but who are from different ethnic backgrounds.

We therefore suggest the term *speech repertoire* for the
repertoire of linguistic varieties utilized by a speech
community which its speakers, as members of the community, may
appropriately use, and the term *verbal repertoire* for the
linguistic varieties which are at a particular speaker's disposal.

Two important concepts which are related to range and type
of repertoire are *access to roles* and *role compartmentalization*.
In more traditional, rigidly stratified speech communities,
access to certain roles (e.g. high positions of employment,
positions of high respect and honour) is severely restricted.
Those whose ancestry is inappropriate cannot attain them,
regardless of their personal achievement.   (Fishman 1971b)
Similarly restricted is the access to certain speech varieties
within these communities.   Members of lower social strata do
not have the opportunity to acquire certain 'higher' speech
varieties, the use of which is linked to those very roles which
are inaccessible to all but the elite.

With role inaccessibility also goes *role compartmentalization*, i.e. the rights and duties that constitute particular
roles are more distinct.   In such communities one also tends to
find marked verbal compartmentalization as well (McCormack 1960).
A speaker whose speech varieties are A, B and C would attempt

ELSEVIER
NORTH-HOLLAND
EXCERPTA MEDICA

Associated Scientific Publishers

P.O. BOX 211
AMSTERDAM
THE NETHERLANDS

Please add my name to your mailing list.

On this card, please mark your specific field(s) of interest, and return to us. Information on new publications of direct importance to you will then be forwarded.

LANGUAGES/LINGUISTICS/LITERATURE

3300 ☐ Linguistics (General)
3310 ☐ Comparative Linguistics
3320 ☐ Semantics
3330 ☐ Computational and Mathematical Linguistics
3340 ☐ Phonetics
3350 ☐ Psycholinguistics
3360 ☐ Socio-linguistics
3410 ☐ Theory of Literature and Poetics
3420 ☐ Russian Literature
3430 ☐ Neo-Latin

Name (please print or type) .... title ....

Institute or company ....

Full address ....

....

....

....

to keep them separate in every way (whether phonologically, lexically or grammatically) just as he would strictly compartmentalize his roles, e.g. as a government minister, the head of a family, a friend.

In modern-type more or less democratic speech communities, there seems to exist a greater fluidity in roles and the speech varieties within a speaker's repertoire, i.e. roles are less strictly defined and an individual can shift from one to the other more easily. Speech varieties too (Fishman 1971b) tend to become more similar as the roles in which they are appropriate become more and more alike.

POINTS FOR DISCUSSION

(1) Gumperz ((1968) 1972:222) states with reference to the 'Romany' used by the gypsies: "They tend to be bilinguals, using their own idiom for in-group communication and the majority language for interaction with outsiders."

(i) What does Gumperz mean by 'majority language'?

(ii) Would you consider the gypsies a speech community

(a) by Gumperz' definition?
(b) by Hymes' definition?

(iii) Can you think of other groups which have one language for in-group communication and one for interaction with outsiders?

(2) Can you think of examples of speech communities where 'access' to certain roles or speech varieties is severely restricted and/or where there is evidence of 'role compartmentalization'?

3.3   *Domains*

In the discussion of speech varieties the concept of *domain* is of importance as it signifies the *class of situations* within which a certain speech variety is used.

Fishman (1971b) defines the three essential ingredients for what he terms 'a social situation' as "the *implementation* of the rights and duties of a particular role relationship, in

the place (locale) most appropriate or most typical for that
relationship, and at *the time* societally defined as appropriate
for that relationship".

For instance, there are situations which could be classed
together under the domain of 'home' (e.g. the family at break-
fast, a family outing, a fight between siblings in the garden)
whereas other situations would belong to the domains of
'school', 'employment', 'church' etc.

The table below shows the optional and obligatory occurrence of social roles (and their variants) within a situation
matrix bounded by a period of social time and an area of social
space (adapted from Bock 1968).

Situation: Class	Time: Class Meeting
Space: Classroom	Roles: + Teacher + Pupil(s) ± Student-Teacher(s)

+ indicates obligatory occurrence

± indicates optional occurrence

When dealing with speech communities and their verbal
repertoires, Fishman (1971b) shows in a table a number of
domains for some of the speech varieties of the communities
investigated:

Societal Domain	Speech Community 1	Speech Community 2	Speech Community 3	Speech Community 4
Home	a_1	c_1	c_1	d_1
School and Culture	a_2	b_3/c_2	b_2/c_2	a_2
Work	a_3	c_3	d_2	d_2
Government	a_2	b_1	a_2	a_2
Church	e_1	b_2	b_2	e_1
	(Moscow, 1960) Russians	(Mea Shearim, 1966) Jews	(Ostropol, 1905) Jews	(Ostropol, 1905) Ukrainians

1-3 signify types of

a = Russian   b = Hebrew   c = Yiddish

d = Ukrainian   e = Church Slavonic

It can be noticed from the table that varieties which are related to one domain in one speech community (e.g. b_2 in SC_2) may be associated with more or different domains in another speech community (e.g. b_2 in SC_3).

Studies of the relationship between speech varieties and certain domains are of vital importance to linguists concerned with the study of bilingualism and multilingualism. (These phenomena will be discussed in detail in Chapter 7).

An interesting bilingual study using 'domains' was made by Greenfield (1972) when measuring normative views concerning the bilingual use of English and Spanish. The test groups were bilingual Puerto Rican youngsters living in New York city. The domains used by Greenfield were: family, friendship, religion, education, employment. The investigation points to various factors, above all, (a) what the speakers themselves *claim* concerning the use of a certain speech variety for certain domains and (b) which factors are more important in reference to their decision making, participants, locale or topic.

POINTS FOR DISCUSSION

(1) Is the concept which Fishman calls 'the social
    situation' identical with what Hymes terms the
    'speech situation'?   Why?   Why not?
    It may be useful to consult section (3) of the
    Fishman article mentioned in the Reading List,
    particularly subsection 4.4. 'The situation:
    congruent and incongruent', as well as Hymes
    (1974) Chapter 2, subsection 'Fundamental
    notions', pp 45-64.

(2) How would you go about ascertaining the speech
    varieties used in a particular speech community
    and for which domain(s) they are used?   Have
    a look at Greenfield's article (1972) mentioned
    earlier.

(3) Read section 4.4 'The situation: congruent
    and incongruent' in the Fishman article on
    The sociology of language (1971b) and discuss
    his definition of incongruent situations.
    How can the parties to the interaction correct
    the incongruency?

(4) Discuss the speech varieties and their domains
    mentioned in Fishman's table on page 39.
    Speech community 2, a special group of ortho-
    dox Jews in Israel, is of particular interest.

EXERCISES

(1) Taking Gumperz' definition of a *speech
    community* can you give further examples
    of groups which you would consider speech
    communities?   Give reasons.

(2) Find out the speech varieties in the verbal
    repertoire of the individual members of
    your family or your group of friends or
    the students in your course.

(3) Specify some situations which could, under
    certain conditions, be classed under the
    domains 'education', 'home', 'employment',
    'religion'.   (In each case, give partici-

pant-roles, place and time).

(4) Give your own examples of what Fishman calls
     'incongruent situations' and explain how
     they could be 'corrected' by the participants.

ASSIGNMENTS

(1) Investigate one speech variety of a small speech
     community,

> e.g. a professional group
>   (legal profession, hairdressers, etc.)
>
> or a group of young people which has
> formed in certain social or cultural
> interaction and possesses a separate
> system of verbal behaviour.

(2) If you are a member of a family group where several
     distinct speech varieties (e.g. languages) are
     used frequently, try to investigate which speech
     varieties are used for which domains.   Maybe you
     could make a distinction of (a) what people claim
     they use and (b) what your own observations on the
     matter are.   It may be of interest to find out
     whether these two aspects coincide.

Greenfield's article (1972) would be useful here.

RECOMMENDED READING

Gumperz J. (1968) 1972.   The speech community.   In *Language
and social context,* P. P. Giglioli ed., 219-231.
Harmondsworth: Penguin.

First published in 1968 in *International encyclopedia
of the social sciences,* 381-386.   Macmillan.

A stimulating article that discusses various aspects
of the speech community.

Fishman J. A. 1971b.   The sociology of language: An inter-
disciplinary social science approach to language in
society.   In *Advances in the sociology of language I,*
J.A. Fishman ed., 217-380.   The Hague: Mouton.

For this particular chapter, sections 3 and 4 would
be the most useful (226-258).

Hymes D. 1972b.   Mentioned in chapter 2.

The following investigations deal with speech variety/
domain relations in bilingual communities:

Greenfield L. 1972.   Situational measures of normative lang-
        uage views.   In *Advances in the sociology of language
        II,* J. A. Fishman ed., 17-33.   The Hague : Mouton.

Findling J. 1972.   Bilingual need affiliation, future orienta-
        tion and achievement motivation.   In *Advances in the
        sociology of language II,*J. A. Fishman ed., 150-174.
        The Hague: Mouton.

CHAPTER 4

4. SOCIOLECTS, STYLES AND REGISTERS

4.0   As mentioned earlier, it is often difficult to decide
whether a speech variety can be classed as a language or just
a dialect of a wider language phenomenon.   A good example is
probably the English language.   Are the speech varieties of
English as spoken in Australia, England, Ireland, New Zealand,
Scotland, South Africa, the U.S.A. etc., separate languages or
just dialects of the same language and if so that criteria are
used to decide this fact?   Suggestions that all these speech
varieties share a common heritage of linguistic structure and
literature have been made, but the problem is a difficult one
because (a) which would be the *standard language* of all the
varieties and (b) what is the attitude of the majority of the
speakers of these varieties to this solution?   Would, for
instance, an American agree that his type of English was just
a 'dialect' of British English?

It has been suggested that dialects are usually speech
varieties pertaining to a particular local region and that
sociolects are speech varieties that signal social status and
educational background and that both types are subvarieties of
a common denominator: the national language.   This may serve
quite well as a vague definition but as will be shown later
(chapter 7), so-called languages can signal social and regional
status and so-called sociolects may also be dialects by the
above definition.

4.1   *Linguistic Variation and Social Factors*

Before the second half of this century, little attention
was paid to that type of variation in speech which is related
to social stratification within a speech community and which is
perceived by the members of this community to exist.   The
relationship between certain linguistic features (e.g. the way
a vowel is realized or the use of a particular syntactic
structure) and the speaker's social background had been perceived for some time.   In general, however, members of a
speech community who were aware of such relationships had a
prescriptive attitude towards them, e.g. 'bad speech, sloppy
speech, lazy speech' as opposed to 'nice speech, educated

speech, refined way of speaking', etc. Linguists were
inclined to shy away, daunted by the complexity of the problems
facing them and the mammoth nature of the task.

Earlier linguistic investigations on dialects had been
mainly carried out in rural regions. As the focus of research
gradually shifted to urban settlements, it was realized that
apart from regional variation there was also a good deal of
social stratification to be considered. Speech varied according to social status or, to be more accurate, according to the
speaker's socio-economic and cultural background.

Social variations in speech could be of a phonetic,
lexical, morphological or syntactic nature, e.g.

(a) phonetic variation

vowels: more or less centralized

$$[\text{a}] \text{ --- } [\wedge]$$

more or less diphthongized

$$[\upsilon] \text{ --- } [\partial\upsilon]$$

consonants:more or less realized

$$[\text{h}] \text{ --- } [\emptyset]$$

fortis to lenis

$$[\text{t}] \text{ --- } [\d{d}]$$

(b) lexical items:

friends ⟷ mates (Australian English)

hotel ⟷ boozer

(c) syntactic (e.g. negation)

I didn't do it ⟷ I never done it

Hammarström (1966, 1975) suggests that all linguistic
units, apart from their 'meaning' -conveying α -function, may
have certain other functions, one of these being what he terms
γ_2 - or sociolectal function, i.e. "properties which charact-
erize groups of speakers (writers) as belonging to particular
social groups". Thus he would speak of 'socio-phones', e.g.
in the case of the realisations $[u]$ (*1) and $[\upsilon]$ (*1) of
phoneme $/\upsilon/$, if these signalled social class difference to the

hearer.

Up to now, the major investigations into sociolectal features have concentrated on phonetic phenomena, but some studies have also been made on variation in lexicon and syntactic structures.

The main problems that arise in sociolectal studies are

(1) How to make accurate statements on sociolectal speech varieties.   Each may be used by vast numbers of speakers.

(2) How to correlate linguistic and social factors.

(3) To what extent is it possible to speak of different 'groups' or 'sociolects' at all? It would be possible simply to give the speaker a place on a scale according to his use or non-use of certain features.   Even if there were 'bunchings' of speakers at certain points of the scale, could one take these as being the 'centres' of distinct sociolects and draw arbitrary lines between them somewhere along the scale - as shown in the diagram below?

```
|
| xx
| xxx        sociolect 1
| xxx
| x
|_____
| x
| xx
| xxxxx      sociolect 2
| xxxx
| xx
| x
|_____
| x
| xx
| xxxx       sociolect 3
| xxx
| xxx
|_____
```

(4) Can one speak at all of the *constant* use of a certain linguistic feature by any one speaker?

For instance, the occurrence or non-occurrence
of ⌈ h ⌉ in word initial positions (e.g. in
'hat') has been recognized as having a sociolectal function.   Do speakers *never* use ⌈ h ⌉
or *always* or do they use it *at certain times*
and not at others?

   We do not wish to give definite answers to the questions
raised but rather look in more detail at two investigations
which have tackled some of the problems raised above in
different ways:

A.   A study by Mitchell and Delbridge (1965) of the Speech
      of Australian Adolescents.   (phonetic aspect only)

Informants: High school students aged 16-18 in government
              and private schools (Catholic and Non-Catholic)

Region: All states of Australia (Canberra, state capitals
          and country centres)

Number of schools: 327.   Number of informants: 7082

Sampling: 25 chosen from each school from form V (every 5th
            name from the class roll)

Recording made by teacher in interview of about three minutes'
conversation.   A variety of topics familiar to the informant
(chosen by the teacher), e.g.:   home, sport, TV, school.

At end of interview: Reading of a word list.

Social variables used: Type of school (Government, Catholic,
non-Catholic) place of birth, sex, region, occupation of father
(9 divisions from professionals to unskilled workers)

Linguistic features: Concentration on six vowels /i,u, ,oʊ
ai,aʊ/ as chief diagnostic features, other factors also considered (but more marginally).

Analysis: Spectrum of diaphones for each vowel was est-
            ablished and the two extremes ascertained.
            After listing and comparing, range of sounds
            was grouped into three varieties:

            e.g. /i/ beat   I   ⌈i⌉ (*2) or ⌈ɪi⌉
                            II   ⌈əɪ⌉
                            III ⌈əᵀ·ɪ⌉

I = Cultivated Australian   II = General Australian

            III = Broad Australian

Speakers were assigned to these three categories (with some misgivings). "Some speakers tended to be consistent and, within certain tolerances, to use set (i) or (ii) or (iii) throughout... some speakers used diaphones from more than one of these sets, and did this to varying extents".

The investigators state: "We resisted the temptation to apply quantative measures derived from counting up the vowels in both varieties in the speech of individuals and fixing on arbitrary qualifying proportions."

The final distribution of informants was

> Broad Australian   2396 (34%)
>
> General Australian   3939 (55%)
>
> Cultivated Australian   747 (11%)

The social factors gathered about the informants were related separately to the three varieties established, e.g.

Schools	Broad	General	Cultivated	Total
State	28	37	3	68 %
Catholic	4	11	3	18 %
Non-Catholic Independent	3	7	4	14 %
	35(*3)	55	10(*3)	100

B.   Labov's Study of Sociolinguistic Variation in New York
     (particularly the Lower East Side)   1964-1966
                      (phonetically based)

Based on primary survey of social attitudes carried out by Mobilization for Youth 1961.

Pre-interview observations, interviews (½ - 1 hr), reading of two standard texts and word lists - classed as Styles A to D.   Investigation of various consonantal and vocalic features, e.g. the variations between

(1)   (th) $[\theta]$ ——— $[t\theta]$ ——— $[t]$ as in 'thing'

     (dh) $[ð]$ ——— $[dð]$ ——— $[d]$ as in 'then'

(2)   The presence or absence of consonantal constriction for post-vocalic, word final and pre-vocalic /r/.

Takes account of speaker's variation in the use of the feature.   For each individual informant, index values are assigned in the following way, e.g. for (th)

0   each time he uses $\left[\theta\right]$

1   each time he uses $\left[t\theta\right]$

2   each time he uses $\left[t\right]$

An index of 00 would mean use of $\left[\theta\right]$ only

An index of 200 would mean use of $\left[t\right]$ only

For a detailed discussion of working with index values, see chapter 6.

The socio-economic index is on a ten-point scale based on occupation (of bread-winner) education (of respondent) income (of family).   This information was taken from the original 1961 survey.

Relationships between the various factors are shown by diagrams such as the class stratification diagrams pp. 49-50.

Two other interesting investigations along similar lines are those of Shuy, Wolfram and Riley on Detroit speech (1967) and Trudgill (1974) on social differentiation of English in Norwich, England.

POINTS FOR DISCUSSION

(1)   How would you go about making representative samplings when investigating the speech of a large group?

(2)   Discuss whether the socio-economic factors used by Mitchell and Delbridge and Labov are suitable ones for their particular investigations.   Why are they?   Why not? Can you think of other factors that should have been included?

(3)   In what way does the Labov investigation differ from that of Mitchell and Delbridge as far as the speaker's use of linguistic features is concerned?

(4)   What are the advantages of divisions of a continuum into different social speech varieties?   What could be disadvantages?

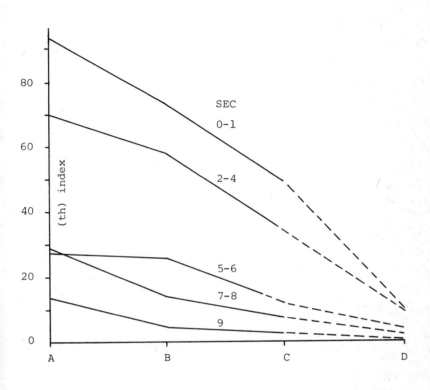

STYLE

Class stratification of a linguistic variable with stable social significance: (th) in thing, through, etc. Socio-economic class scale: 0-1, lower class; 2-4, working class; 5-6, 7-8, lower middle class; 9, upper middle class. A, casual speech; B, careful speech; C, reading style; D, word lists.

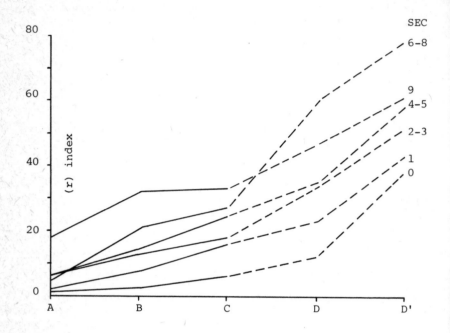

STYLE

    Class stratification of a linguistic variable in
process of change: (r) in guard, car, beer, beard,
board, etc. SEC (Socio-economic class) scale: 0-1,
lower class;   2-4, working class;   5-6, 7-8, lower
middle class;   9, upper middle class.   A, casual
speech;   B, careful speech;   C, reading style;
D, world lists;   D', minimal pairs.

4.2   *Relationship between Sociolects and Regional Dialects*

In many countries, it is not possible to view sociolectal
and dialectal variations in isolation.   Seen from the point
of view of social stratification, linguists have claimed that
there is often a close integration between the two in the way
that the higher the speaker's sociolect, the fewer features of
a regional dialect would be detectable in his speech.   This
phenomenon has been explained as due, in part, to the greater
mobility of the upper social classes as compared to many of the
other levels of the community.

However, one should take this view with caution.   No
doubt, it is true in many cases but there are other points to
be considered.   If economic factors in certain rural areas
forced small farmers to work in the factories of the urban
centres, then not only would their strong regional dialect
features be disparaged by the urban factory workers but their
variety of regional speech would gradually be looked upon as a
sub-variety of working class speech in the urban area.   There
are, however, cases where, because of pride in the region,
speakers deliberately adhere to certain strong regional
features.   These speakers may be (but not necessarily are)
considered 'archaic' but they would on the whole not speak a
'low' sociolect as they may comprise prosperous farmers and
small town shop-keepers.

Furthermore, the degree of regional-free sociolectal
variation varies from speech community to speech community.
In more recently settled countries like Australia, the regional
variations between the various states are not very great in any
case.   If there is a noticeable regional difference, it is
more between older generations in rural areas and the urban
population in general.   In England, the highest sociolect, RP
(Received Pronunciation English) appears to be virtually free
of regional features but this is not the case in Germany where,
particularly in colloquial speech patterns, the higher sociolects show definite features signalling the speaker's regional
background.

POINTS FOR DISCUSSION

(1)   Discuss what is the relation in your speech
      community between sociolectal and dialectal
      variations.   Do regional dialects form an
      integral part of the sociolectal system of
      your speech community?   In what way?

(2)   Can you think of examples from any country

where upper sociolects show a high degree
of regional variation?

4.3 Attitudes to Sociolectal Variations

Most people have likes and dislikes concerning certain
sociolects. Some dislike upper sociolects and claim that they
are 'put on, snobbish', etc. Some dislike lower sociolects
and claim that they sound 'coarse, ugly, harsh', etc. Such
attitudes are based either on the attitudes people have to the
speakers of these sociolects or on certain prescriptive views
concerning language which were acquired at school or in the
home.

Negative attitudes to certain pronunciations are often
highly emotive and irrational. In Australia, for instance,
the use of $\begin{bmatrix} ɔ^ɪ \end{bmatrix}$ for $\begin{bmatrix} a^ɪ \end{bmatrix}$ in 'wine' in lower sociolects has
been attacked by the statement that $\begin{bmatrix} ɔ^ɪ \end{bmatrix}$ is an 'ugly sound'.
However, it is perfectly acceptable in many speech varieties of
English in $\begin{bmatrix} b ɔ^ɪ \end{bmatrix}$ 'boy'.

Likewise, the glottal stop used in some varieties of
English, e.g. Cockney, has been termed 'an ugly sound used by
low, common people'. However, the glottal stops produced in
the high sociolects of Arabic, Malay and German are considered
perfectly respectable and acceptable to members of these speech
communities.

This does not mean, of course, that one should wipe aside
attitudes to speech varieties as 'prejudiced rubbish not worthy
of consideration'. Testing attitudes to speech varieties, e.g.
sociolects, can be of great value to explain apparently un-
reasonable hostility to an individual or a group, e.g. when
investigating tensions in factories and workshops, and in mixed-
social-group schools, attitudes by students to a teacher or
lecturer, attitudes of employees to the 'boss' etc.

Quite a number of 'attitude' tests to certain languages,
dialects or sociolects have been carried out.

In 1967 Tucker and Lambert (1972) played samples of
recorded speech of representatives of six American-English
'dialect' groups (network, Educated White Southern, Educated
Negro Southern, Mississippi Peer, Howard University, New York
Alumni) to three groups of college students (one Northern
White, one Southern White and one Southern Negro). The informants were asked to evaluate certain characteristics of the
speakers, using an adjective checklist. The rating scales
were chosen with two ends in mind

(a)   positive ratings should show that the
       listener believes the speakers could
       attain or have attained 'success'   and

(b)   that speakers are 'friendly'

In pilot studies, bipolar rating scales were constructed
for each group of listeners (with the assistance of the
listener test group) pairing a positive and a negative adjective with each trait (e.g. good upbringing - poor upbringing,
considerate - inconsiderate, etc.)

The *Network* speakers were judged most favourably by both
Northern Whites and Southern Negro listeners, next in line was
Educated Negro Southern.   The Southern White students also
ranked the *Network* speakers first but gave *Educated White
Southern* the second place.

Speakers do not necessarily judge their own sociolect as
the best but may prefer a prestige sociolect although they
themselves do not use it.   On the other hand, speakers could
be proud of their own social variety, although it is considered
a low sociolect by others, and despise higher sociolects as
'the boss's language'.

POINTS FOR DISCUSSION

(1)   To what extent have prescriptive attitudes
       at school or at home influenced your
       attitude towards certain speech varieties?

(2)   Consider whether, when conducting attitude
       tests with recorded material, there are any
       additional factors which could affect the
       judgement of the listener and cloud the
       issue, e.g. the listener may be irritated
       by the personal quality of the speaker's
       voice.   Can you think of other examples?

(3)   If a member of a speech community moved from
       one social sphere to the next, would he or she
       be able to change sociolect (soon, after some
       time, never)?   On what factors would this
       depend?

4.4   *Functional Varieties and Styles*

Some American sociolinguists seem to favour the use of
the term *functional variety* when investigating the relationship

between speech varieties and certain domains.   The term *style*
is often used to signify a variation in speech (or writing)
from more formal to more casual.   Some sociolinguists like
Labov stress the continuum aspect of stylistic variation, i.e.
certain linguistic variables change as the speech gets more or
less informal;   others, like Ervin-Tripp stress the correct
application of co-occurrence rules, e.g. a more formal style
would have more complex syntactic structures, a more elaborate
range of lexicon and more careful attention to phonetic realization than would, for example, a very casual style, e.g. in
American English (Ervin-Tripp 1969)

> (Style 1)   What are you doing?
>
> (Style 2)   Whaddya doin ?
>
> (Style 3)   Whach doon ?

Style would vary according to the speech situation.   A
more formal style would be used at ceremonies, public functions,
formal discussions, whereas a more casual style would be more
appropriate for conversation with friends, fellow students or
at home.

Another way of looking at style is to consider a certain
'bunching together' of linguistic items (e.g. phonological,
lexical, grammatical) to form distinct 'stylistic groups' which
function in certain social contexts, e.g. Joos (1968) specifies
that "the number of groups must be finite, preferably rather
small" and suggests five styles:

> 1.   intimate
>
> 2.   casual
>
> 3.   consultative
>
> 4.   formal
>
> 5.   frozen

A switch from one style to the next can occur within one
speech event, e.g. from casual to consultative (in a conversation between neighbours) from casual to intimate (between two
friends).

Markers for a more casual style in some varieties of
English would be e.g.

The absence of an article at the beginning of a sentence

> Friend of mine saw it.
> Coffee's cold!

The absence of the subject at the beginning of a sentence

Bought it yesterday.
Makes no difference.

The absence of an auxiliary

Leaving?
Seen John lately?

Some markers for the formal style would be

The use of 'may' (instead of 'might' and 'can') and constructions such as "For whom did you get it?" instead of "Who'd you get it for?" in more casual speech.

POINTS FOR DISCUSSION

(1) In what way do the concepts of 'style' of Labov, Ervin-Tripp and Joos differ and in what way do they show similarities? You may like to consult the appropriate references for a more fruitful discussion of this topic, i.e. Labov (1972: 70-109) 'The isolation of contextual styles', Ervin-Tripp ((1969)1971) 'Sociolinguistics', particularly section C, pp 38-43, and Joos (1968: 185-191).

(2) Can styles be mixed deliberately and drastically in the one speech situation? What effects could be achieved by doing so?
Example: In a formal discussion in the boardroom, one of the directors drops suddenly into a very casual style.

4.5 *Registers and Styles*

Some American and British linguists use *register* in a very restricted sense, i.e. referring to occupational speech varieties which are characterized primarily by their variation in lexicon: "since different topics are required in different milieux" (Ervin-Tripp 1969).

However, Halliday, McIntosh and Strevens (1964) use *register* as a wider concept, more in the way in which many American sociolinguists use 'functional variety'. "When we observe language activity in the various contexts in which it

takes place, we find differences in the type of language
selected as appropriate to different types of situation".
They see the greatest variation in registers mainly in the
lexical items and grammatical features, e.g. in advertising,
church services, sports commentaries, and they consider
registers not as marginal or special varieties but as "covering
the whole range of our language activity".

Three dimensions are suggested for the classification of
registers:

      (a)   field of discourse

      (b)   mode of discourse

      (c)   style of discourse

(a)   *Field of discourse* refers to the area of operation of the
language activity. Registers classified according to field
of discourse may include shopping and games playing as well as
medicine and linguistics.

(b)   *Mode of discourse* has as its main distinction the
division into written and spoken language but finer distinctions are possible.

(c)   *Style of discourse* refers to the relation among the
participants. This is shown in speech by a variation between
colloquial and polite styles.

For instance, a lecture on biology in a technical college
could be identified as

     field: scientific (biological)

     mode :   oral (academic lecturing)

     style: polite (teacher —— student style)

POINTS FOR DISCUSSION

(1)   If you take the narrow definition of *register*
     as 'referring to occupational speech varieties'
     - is it correct to say that registers 'vary in
     lexicon only'? What about the language of
     the legal profession when contrasted with some
     other occupational variety? Is the difference
     only in lexicon or also in syntax?

(2)   Halliday, McIntosh and Strevens, although con-
     ceding that some registers have distinctive

features at other levels, see the crucial
criteria of any register in its grammar and
lexicon.   Do you agree?

(3)   Is the *field of discourse* discussed in
Halliday et al. identical to the *domain*
discussed in chapter 3?   Why?   Why not?

(4)   Is the concept of 'style' discussed in
Halliday et al. wider or narrower than
the concepts used by Labov, Ervin-Tripp
and Joos?

4.6   *Bernstein's Eleborated and Restricted Codes*

A special case of linking different styles with social
class can be seen in the theory of the educational sociologist
B. Bernstein of the existence and use of the 'elaborated code'
and the 'restricted code'.   The linking by Bernstein of these
'codes' to social class made them appear to some linguists
like a type of social dialect.   Bernstein appeared (*4) to
claim that working class children had little or no access to
the 'elaborated code' thus missing out on the ability to
express themselves fully on certain topics and being disadvantaged in the school situation where this code was mainly used.

(It must be understood that this is a somewhat over-
simplified rendering of Bernstein's views which were modified
by him in some of his later writings.)

Bernstein's statements were followed not only by an upsurge of so-called 'compensatory education' but also by a
number of writings for and against his theory (e.g. for:
Oevermann 1969, Halliday 1973;   against: Labov 1969, Jäger
1972, Bartsch 1973).

When one looks at the two 'codes', they appear far more
like *styles* than *sociolects*.   The 'elaborated code' is
characterized by the frequent use of the pronoun 'I', and is
said to contain a large number of adjectives, passive constructions, conjunctions and subordinate clauses whereas the
'restricted code' uses more the pronouns 'you' and 'they' and
shows, in general, absence of the features mentioned above
under 'elaborated code'.   In Bernstein's own words (1970):
"elaborated codes orient their users towards universalistic
meanings, whereas restricted codes orient, sensitize, their
users to particularistic meanings".

If one considers that in many speech communities a

speaker's range of stylistic variation is tied to his sociolect, one could agree that some sociolects do not make use of
certain stylistic varieties which are used by others - but
whether

(a)   certain varieties are 'better' than others and should
       be acquired by all speakers of the community and
       whether

(b)   speakers who do not possess these stylistic varieties
       are unable to express their thoughts and ideas
       adequately - that is quite another matter.

DISCUSSION

     Read the two articles by Bernstein suggested
in the Reading List and discuss

     (a) whether or not his views have
          changed

     (b) whether or not you agree with
          his views on the whole.

In conclusion, three points need to be stressed

(a) When using such terms as register and style, it is wise
to define one's concept of them for any particular investigation.

(b) As Labov, Trudgill and others have realized, one has to
see speech in context as an interaction between social variety
and stylistic variety (meaning here the variation from casual
to more formal speech).

(c) Just as there are varying degrees of interaction between
sociolects and dialects in speech communities, so there are
between sociolects and stylistic variations. On the whole one
can say that stylistic variation moves within a speaker's
particular sociolect, i.e. that what is often referred to as
'sociolect switching' is in reality 'switching of stylistic
varieties'. Exceptions to this would be speech communities
which use their sociolectal varieties as stylistic varieties
and where at least the speakers of the upper sociolects might
have the whole sociolectal spectrum at their disposal for
functional (stylistic) use (See DeCamp 1971b, Day 1973 and
Platt 1975b).

EXERCISES

(We shall use the concept of 'style' as meaning variation from casual to more formal speech or
writing).

(1) Make a list of the vowels and
consonants in the speech of the
members of your speech community
which you would consider to be
'sociophones', i.e. functioning
as indicators of the speaker's
social status.

(2) Make a list of lexical items that
would show sociolectal variations
in your language.

(3) Make a list of lexical items which
would show stylistic variations
within your own speech (e.g.
recuperate - get better).

(4) Sociolinguistic investigations of
youngsters usually concentrate
on father's occupation, income and
social status. Why is mother's
occupation and mother's educational
background ignored?
Give some reasons for or against the
inclusion of information about the
child's mother.

(5) Make a list of some social or
regional varieties or even languages
that people say they like or dislike
and find out some of the reasons for
these attitudes.

(6) Examine some of the informal and
formal styles used by the members
of your family or your friends and
try to isolate at least one phonological variable, a small group of
lexical variables and one or two
syntactic variables.

(7) Not only foreigners but also native
speakers use at times a stylistic

variety in an inappropriate situation.   Give examples.

ASSIGNMENTS

(1) Take a small sampling from a small group of
     people (e.g. the street where you live, a
     society or association you belong to).
     Record your informants
                              (a) reading a text

                              (b) in a casual interview

          (see Appendix 'Field Methods')

     (i)   Choose two vowels and two con-
           sonants and investigate whether
           each individual speaker varies
           these features between (a) and
           (b).

     (ii) If you wish, work out and
           tabulate the frequencies in the
           way Labov did (see also chapter
           6 for further information on his
           method).

     (iii) Show in what way your informants
           differ from one another in their
           use of the four phonetic features.

(2) Record eight speakers, four from what is
     generally considered an upper social group and
     four from what is generally considered a lower
     social group (the greater the social difference
     the better).   Use an even mixture of upper and
     lower class listeners and adopt a similar
     approach to Tucker and Lambert (1972) mentioned
     earlier.

RECOMMENDED READING

Sociolectal Investigations

Labov   W. 1972d.   The reflection of social processes.   In
         Sociolinguistic patterns, W. Labov ed., 110-121.
         Philadelphia: University of Pennsylvania Press.

         A more detailed account can be found in 1966.
         The social stratification of English in New York City.

Washington D.C.:   Center for Applied Linguistics.

Mitchell A. G. and Delbridge A.   1965.   *The speech of Australian adolescents*.   Sydney: Angus and Robertson.

Trudgill P.   1974.   *The social differentiation of English in Norwich*.   London: Cambridge University Press.

Investigation into Attitudes to Speech Varieties

Tucker   R. G. and Lambert W. E.   1972.   White and negro listeners' reactions to various American English dialects.   In *Advances in the sociology of language II*, J. A. Fishman ed., 175-184.   The Hague: Mouton.

Registers and Styles

Halliday M. A. K., McIntosh A. and Strevens P.   1964.   *The linguistic sciences and language teaching*.   London: Longmans, Green & Co.   The particular chapter referred to is Chapter 4 'The users and uses of language' which can also be found in *Readings in the sociology of language*, J. A. Fishman, ed., 139-169.   The Hague: Mouton.

Ervin-Tripp S.   (1969) 1971.   Mentioned in the Reading List in Chapter 2.

Joos   M.   1968.   The isolation of styles.   In *Readings in the sociology of language*, J. A. Fishman ed., 185-191.   The Hague: Mouton.

Labov   W.   1972c.   The isolation of contextual styles.   In *Sociolinguistic patterns*, W. Labov ed. 70-109.   Philadelphia: University of Pennsylvania Press.

Elaborated Code and Restricted Code

Bernstein B.   1964.   Elaborated and restricted codes: their social origins and some consequences.   In *The Ethnography of communication*, J. Gumperz and D. Hymes, eds., 55-69.   Washington D.C. American Anthropological Association.

(1970) 1972.   Social class, language and social-
ization.   In *Language and social context*, P. P.
Giglioli ed., 156-178.   Harmondsworth: Penguin.

An argument against Bernstein and some of his interpreters
is given in

Labov   W. (1969) 1972.   The logic of nonstandard English.
In *Language and social context*, P. P. Giglioli ed.,
179-215.   Harmondsworth: Penguin.

A fuller version of the article can be found in the
Georgetown Monographs on Language and Linguistics, vol. 22,
1969, 1-22 and 26-31.

Footnotes

(*1)   [ɯ̄] = unrounded close back vowel

          [ʊ̄] = rounded half close back vowel

(*2)   The writers consider this to be an unlikely realization
          for *any* variety of Australian English.

(*3)   There appears to be a discrepancy of 1% in the overall
          Broad and Cultivated categories when compared with the
          figures given above.

(*4)   Bernstein claimed later that he had been misinterpreted
          by a number of writers.   For arguments against this
          claim see Jäger (1972).

CHAPTER 5

5.   AGE AND SEX AS SOCIOLINGUISTIC VARIABLES

5.1 *The Age Variable*

     It has been noticed that in many speech communities the
speech of the older generation varies from that of the younger
generation in certain ways.   This does not mean that older
people have an entirely different speech variety.   Mostly it
is a matter of certain linguistic features which can *only* be
found in the speech of the older members of the group, or
features which are *more frequently* used by the older members.
Younger members may still use them but only in writing whereas
the older generation still uses them in oral communication.
Conversely, one can find linguistic features in the speech of
the younger generation which are absent or infrequent in the
speech of the older members.

     One can compare this type of variation to some extent with
some sociolectal variations but this phenomenon can be seen on
a different axis, often cutting across social stratification,
as shown in the diagram below:

6-20	20-40	40-60	60-80
	social class C		
	social class B		
	social class A		

     These observations are very useful to sociolinguists
investigating linguistic change in a certain speech community.

     When, for instance, a certain linguistic feature is
gradually becoming more and more a prestige marker, one would
expect members of the older generation to be more conservative

and keep to the older form whereas the younger generation could
be expected to use the new feature more frequently.

This has been shown to be partially correct by Labov (1966,
1972) when investigating the case of 'post-vocalic /r/' which
was only recently introduced as a prestige marker into the
speech of New York City.   As Labov points out, certain other
factors apart from age play a part in the acceptance of the new
feature, e.g. insecurity and 'prestige consciousness' of some
(particularly older) members of the lower middle class.

Recordings were made of various speakers reading a para-
graph containing the feature tested (in this case /r/) and
each listener was asked to place the speaker on an 'occupational
suitability scale'.   (For further details of this investigation
in general and the testing method in particular see Labov 1972:
143-159).

The table below (adapted from Labov 1972) shows the
percentages of (r)-positive response for two age levels (20-39
and over 40) and five divisions of the socio-economic scale.
(0-1:   lower class, 2-4:   working class, 5-6, 7-8:   lower
middle class, 9:   upper middle class)

Age	0-1	2-3	4-5	6-8	9	Total
20-39	100	100	100	100	100	100
40-	63	67	50	70	57	62

DISCUSSION

It has been suggested in the Labov investigation
of New York City speech that a certain 'insecurity'
of some members of the lower middle class had an
effect on the results obtained.   In what way could
that be possible?   Give your own views.   You may
also like to check up in Labov (1972, Chapter 5)
for his views on the matter.

5.3   *The Sex Variable*

Many linguists investigating linguistic variation in
social context in recent years have found another interesting

variable: i.e. difference in use of certain linguistic
features between men and women of the same social class (e.g.
Labov 1966 and 1972 on New York City speech, Trudgill 1974 on
the speech patterns of Norwich, England and the Detroit study
of Shuy, Wolfram and Riley 1967).

It is only recently that there has been a systematic
inclusion of the 'sex variable' in linguistic analysis.   This
does not mean, of course, that variation in verbal behaviour
between men and women had not previously been noticed by a
number of linguists but usually the phenomenon had been discussed only in casual, rather brief comments or observations.
If a more systematic approach to variation in male/female
verbal behaviour was made, it appeared in the works of anthropologists and sociologists rather than linguists.

The types of variation that can occur range from differences in the use of phonetic features to the use of different
lexical items and syntactic-semantic structures.   Beyond that,
we can also observe a difference in permissible sequencing of
utterances, even a variation in a temporal aspect, e.g. when to
speak and when to be silent.   The following arrangement of a
number of investigations under levels of analysis has been
chosen as a convenient way of presenting the material.   It
must be understood that, in many instances, male/female
differences on several linguistic levels can be observed con-
currently in any one speech community.

A.   *Phonetic Differences*

(1)   In some speech communities, women's vowels are more
fronted than those of men.   Often women utter certain vowels
with greater lip rounding than males.   Sometimes consonants
are more fronted too.   This is the case in some Western Desert
Aboriginal languages of Australia where the consonant usually
notated either as /tj/ or /ty/ is lamino-dental with women but
lamino-alveolar with men.

(2)   In the survey of speech of Australian adolescents
mentioned in Chapter 4 (Mitchell and Delbridge 1965), the
distribution of the boys in the vowel spectrum was found to
differ significantly from that of the girls.   Most of the boys
were found to be in the Broad or General categories.   The
proportion of girls classed under Cultivated Australian was
about 8 times that of boys as can be seen from the table on
page 66 (adapted from Mitchell and Delbridge 1965:39)

	Broad	General	Cultivated	Total
Males	24	22	1	47
Females	10	33.5	9.5	53

No systematic 'language attitude' survey was carried out but when the topic of attitude to speech came up in the interview, it appeared that boys were quite content with their type of Australian speech and even hostile to the view that another speech variety might be more advantageous to them.

(3)   In Norwich, England, velar nasal (ng) in suffixes such as walk*ing*, laugh*ing*, was identified as one of the variables in an investigation into speech patterns of social varieties (Trudgill 1972) i.e. 'ing' could be pronounced $[\text{I}\eta]$ or $[\partial\text{n}\sim\text{ŋ}]$. Using Labov-type index scores, Trudgill allotted one point for each realization of $[\text{I}\eta]$ and 2 points for the realization $[\partial\text{n}\sim\text{ŋ}]$. The sums of these scores were divided by the total number of instances. The value of 1 was subtracted from this mean score and the result multiplied by 100. This gives an index score of 000 for consistent use of $[\text{I}\eta]$ and 100 for consistent use of $[\partial\text{n}\sim\text{ŋ}]$.

The tabulated index scores for five social classes and four varieties of style show a considerable difference between male and female speakers. It appears that women on the whole use the more prestigious form (in this case $[\text{I}\eta]$ more frequently than men. See the table on page 67 (Trudgill 1972: 182).

(4)   When discussing intonation patterns of American English, Brend (1971) states that although some of these patterns have been discussed very fully (e.g. Pike 1945), little attention has been given to the differences between the intonation of males and females. She suggests, for instance, that certain patterns are absent from men's speech (or far less frequently used), e.g.

The 'unexpectedness' and 'surprise' patterns of high-low downglides as

'Oh   'that's   'awful !

		Style			
Class	Sex	WLS	RPS	FS	CS
MMC	M	000	000	004	031
	F	000	000	000	000
LMC	M	000	020	027	017
	F	000	000	003	067
UWC	M	000	018	081	095
	F	011	013	068	077
MWC	M	024	043	091	097
	F	020	046	081	088
LWC	M	060	100	100	100
	F	017	054	097	100

Styles: Word List, Reading Passage, Formal Speech,
               Casual Speech

Social Class: Middle Middle Class, Lower Middle Class,
               Upper Working Class, Middle Working Class,
               Lower Working Class.

In some cases, there is a difference in the length of the upstep, e.g. men tend to use patterns that show a small upstep from low,

'Yes 'yes, I 'know

whereas women prefer a 'more polite' incomplete longer upstep

'yes 'yes I 'know.

The writers have found that certain intonation patterns are more frequently used by Australian females (particularly of Working or Middle Class origin) than by males. One is a regular final rise in statements, e.g.

I like shopping here.   I can get everything I want.

And everything is so fresh...

There is also overall a greater range of pitch from high to low in female intonation than in that of most males.

DISCUSSION

It seems to be more common for girls to attend speech training lessons. Why would this be so? Do you think that, under certain circumstances, speech training lessons *could* have an influence on speech? Should girls *and* boys have speech training lessons? Or only girls? Or nobody at all? Give arguments for your views.

B.   *Lexical Variation*

(1)   In Australian English there is a difference in the use of words such as boy(s) and girl(s). It has been claimed that girl/woman are semantically exclusive (though that is not so in every case). Seen in context, the matter is certainly much more complex.

girl

(a)   A woman often uses 'girl' when referring to a third person (a woman up to and usually including middle age), e.g.

The girl over the way should be on the kindergarten committee too.

whereas a man would usually refer to her as 'woman'
(particularly if she was middle-aged) - unless he was
having an affair with her and considered her particularly
youthful and desirable.

(b)   In addressing another woman, a woman would only use
'girl' in a patronizing way in either a fixed or
temporary superior role relationship, e.g. older
relative to young housewife

My dear girl, I told you to keep an eye on
that roast!

(c)   As an address form 'girls' is commonly used by females
to females of all ages.

Come along girls, let's get on with the
discussion!

(This could be said at a senior citizens' club).
Men would mainly use 'ladies' in these situations,
although 'girls' is sometimes used by some 'chummy-
chummy' male TV personalities.

boy

Men frequently use 'boys' ('the boys') to refer to
their group of male friends. It could be used
jokingly by a wife when referring to her husband's
friends but hardly by a female when referring to
her male friends.

(2)   Robin Lakoff (1973:45-80) makes some interesting observations in her article 'Language and woman's place'.

(a)   Women have far more precise discriminations in naming
colours than men have. A man may consider as
'purple' or 'a light shade of purple' something which
could be 'mauve, lilac, lavender or purple' to a
woman.

(b)   There is a whole range of evaluative adjectives in
English, the users of which would be predominantly
women, e.g. 'adorable, charming, sweet, lovely, divine'
(and the writers would like to add 'darling' when used
as an adjective, e.g. 'I've just bought a darling
puppy').

C. *Patterns of Communication*

(1)   There are rules in certain societies regarding when to
speak and when to be silent.   These often vary according to
sex, e.g. in the Araucanian speech community (American Indians
in Chile), men are encouraged to talk on all occasions but the
ideal woman is silent in her husband's presence.   At gatherings where men are present, she only talks in whispers or
hardly at all (Hymes 1974).

In Westernized societies, general rules about times of
silence (e.g. at a church service, in the cinema, etc.) are
bi-sexual - but there are cases where women's verbal behaviour
is (or at least was) more strictly controlled.   For instance,
in certain social classes a woman's reaction to a risqué joke
told in her presence in mixed company had to be 'icy silence'
or, if she laughed at all, it had to be a short, soft discreet
laugh.   Lengthy guffaws were out of the question, although
not considered wrong for men of the same social background in
similar situations.

(2)   Not only is there a difference between the structuring
and contents of speech events of different nations;   there is
also a difference between males and females of the same speech
community in the usual structuring of certain events.

For instance, in some varieties of English the 'weather
dialogue' is usually introduced in shopping situations by the
salesman/saleswoman *after* the purchase has been made as a type
of contact making and 'decommercializing' of the transaction.
This dialogue is far more frequent between Saleswoman (SF) and
Female Customer (CF) than in any other combination.   It occurs
less frequently in either SM (Salesman)/CF or SM/CM (Male
Customer) situations and very rarely in SF/CM situations.

Often there is a different structuring and a difference in
length of the permitted sequence, e.g.

SM/CM	SF/CF
SM: Nice weather, we're having today.	SF: Hasn't it been a lovely day today?
CM: (r_1 - final)	CF: (r_1 - often non-final indicated by CF's action and intonation pattern)
	SF: ....
	CF: (r_2 - usually final)

SF: ....

CF: $(r_3$ - final)

r = response

If in certain SF/CF shopping situations, CF adopted the male pattern shown on the left, it could be construed as 'rude' by SF.   If, on the other hand, CM adopted the female pattern, it would usually be considered 'odd' by SM.

POINTS FOR DISCUSSION

(1)   Can one talk of a 'purely-semantic' approach to lexical items, i.e. view them entirely in isolation without referring to their usage? How valuable is this?   Before discussing this point you may like to define first *your* concept of 'semantic'.

(2)   Can you think of other groups of adjectives in English (or in another language) which have 'female-orientated' subgroups?

(3)   Why do you think that the verbal behaviour of women in certain societies (such as the Araucanian) is so highly regulated?

(4)   Is there any difference in your speech community (or other speech communities you know of) between female and male communication patterns?   For instance, are there occasions when men may talk but females have to be silent (or vice versa)?   Are there particular speech patterns, e.g. type of sequencing which are exclusively (or mostly) used by females?

5.3   *Dyalŋuy*

A special case of the male/female - younger/older generation division is the 'taboo' language of some communities.   This is often based on complex kinship relations.   An interesting example is the so-called 'mother-in-law' language of the Dyirbal tribe in North Queensland, Australia (Dixon 1971).

Every user of Dyirbal has two distinct speech varieties

Guwal (the every-day language)   and
Dyalŋuy (the 'mother-in-law' language).

Dyalŋuy is used when certain 'taboo' relatives are present or
nearby. For a woman, the father-in-law was taboo, for the man,
the mother-in-law, and also father's sister's daughter and
mother's brother's daughter.

Guwal and Dyalŋuy phonology are identical and they are
nearly identical in grammar but their vocabularies are completely different - not a single lexical item is common to
Djalŋuy and Guwal;   e.g.
(Dixon 1971:437)

Guwal	*Dyalŋuy*
nudin 'cut deeply, sever'	
gunban 'cut less deeply, cut a piece out'	d^{y}alŋgan - 'cut'

5.4   *Some final comments*

Various reasons have been advanced for the variation in
the speech of females and males. All are still speculative
as little concrete evidence has as yet been produced.

It has been suggested that women are more status conscious
and more sensitive to the linguistic markers which signal
prestige. It has also been suggested (Labov 1966) that working class speech, at least in some Western societies, has a
certain ruggedness about it and that these attributes of rough-
ness and toughness are considered to be male rather than female
attributes.

There is no doubt that, in many societies, woman's role
has been considered a different one from that of the male.
In some societies, it appears to have been a rather subservient
role - in others, such as Western nations, it has been one of
varying status. Often, but not always, there has been a
marked dichotomy between a concept of 'female' (more refined,
gentle, amiable and more sensitive to aesthetic values) and a
concept of 'male' (more rugged, energetic, aggressive and
dynamic). This has certainly made its mark on the overall
speech patterns of many Western societies, e.g. the more
refined speech is often the more prestigious speech, the
greater attention to detail (e.g. colour divisions) is often a
female attribute. The deliberately rugged, more careless

approach to speech and speech patterns would fit more into the concept of 'male'.   Societal pressures have no doubt exaggerated the male-female dichotomy unnecessarily.

An interesting and appropriate approach for finding out how women and men judge their own speech and the speech of others is the conducting of 'attitude tests' in which, by means of a variety of techniques, informants are encouraged to evaluate speech patterns.   If these or additional tests also elicited *why* certain attitudes were held by the informants, this would be of great value indeed.

DISCUSSION

How do you account for some of the differences between the speech patterns of males and females? Give your own reasons.   Then read Labov (1972, Chapter 9, subsection: the role of women), Trudgill (1972) and R. Lakoff (1973) - all quoted in the Reading List - and discuss to what extent you agree or disagree with the views put forward there.

EXERCISES

(1)   Make a list of differences in the pronunciation of vowel sounds and/or
consonant sounds that you notice between
women and men in your speech community.

(2)   Are there any differences in your speech
community between male and female
intonation patterns?   If there are,
list some of them.

(3)   Make a short list of commonly used word
pairs such as boy/girl, woman/man,
lady/gentleman, Madam/Sir, and investigate the difference between male and
female usage.   You would have to define
to some extent the speech situation and
the participant roles.

(4)   Robin Lakoff (1973:51) claims that the
following adjectives, when used to
indicate the speaker's approbation or
admiration for something, are 'neutral'

as to sex of speaker and that either men
or women may use them:

        great, terrific, cool, neat

Would this statement be true for women of
all age groups? Construct a simple test
to find the answer.

ASSIGNMENT

Observe similar situations which involve greetings and leave takings between

(a) 2 females

(b) 2 males

(c) 1 male and 1 female

Analyse the difference.

RECOMMENDED READING

Labov   W. (1966) 1972. Hypercorrection by the lower middle
class as a factor of linguistic change.   In
Sociolinguistic patterns, W. Labov ed., 122-142.
Philadelphia : University of Pennsylvania Press.

First published 1966 in *Sociolinguistics,* W. Bright
ed.   The Hague : Mouton.

This contains several interesting points on male-
female differences.

Labov   W. 1972.   Subjective dimensions of a linguistic
change in progress.   In *Sociolinguistic patterns,*
W. Labov ed., 143-159.   Philadelphia : University
of Pennsylvania Press.

Gives details of 'occupational suitability' tests to
evaluate attitudes to linguistic prestige markers.

Lakoff   R. 1973.   Language and woman's place.   In *Language
in society,* 2, 48-80.

Trudgill P. 1972.   Sex, covert prestige and linguistic change
in the urban British English of Norwich.   In *Language
in society,* 1, 179-195.

6. LANGUAGE CHANGE AND ITS SOCIAL MOTIVATION

6.0 *Earlier barriers to research on language change in progress*

Although it has long been accepted that languages change, it is only fairly recently that attempts have been made at examining this change *in progress.*

Labov, whose name is particularly associated with research on linguistic change in progress, mentions three restrictions or barriers to such research (1972):

(1) "Saussure had enunciated the principle that structural systems of the present and historical changes of the past had to be studied in isolation."

(2) It was asserted that "sound changes could not in principle be directly observed."

(3) "free variation could not in principle be constrained."

Saussure's insistence on the separation of synchrony (the description of language as viewed at one point in time) and diachrony (the description of language change considered over a period of time) was a reaction against certain types of dia-chronic descriptions. Saussure's maxims caused a general reaction against any type of diachronic investigation and particularly of diachronic explanations of synchronic facts.

The second barrier mentioned by Labov refers to the observation of Bloomfield (1933) that any fluctuations which one might observe would only be cases of dialect borrowing and Hockett's observation (1958) that sound change was too slow to be observed while structural change was too fast.

The third restriction mentioned by Labov is perhaps the most important. Linguists allowed for free variation but, as implied by the term, these variations were felt to be of no linguistic significance. Thus, if on one occasion a vowel should be realized in a more open form than on another this was taken to be of no interest unless there was some conditioning factor, e.g. positional variants.

6.1   *Labov's investigation on Martha's Vineyard*

Labov's investigation of a sound change on the island of
Martha's Vineyard off the coast of Massachusetts, U.S.A.
(1963) not only illustrates a sound change in progress but
offers a social motivation for that change.   Labov was able
to compare his findings with the records of the Linguistic
Atlas of New England (Kurath, et al. 1941).   There was a
period of over 30 years between the field work for that work
and Labov's investigation.

He deals with the two diphthongs /ay/ and /aw/ which he
refers to as the linguistic variables (ay) and (aw), and from
a sample of 69 speakers, somewhat more than 1 percent of the
population, he investigated the degree of centralization of
these diphthongs on a 4 point scale.   From the 69 informants
he obtained 3,500 instances of the /ay/ diphthong and 1,500
instances of the less frequently occurring /aw/.   The standard
New England form of /ay/ is [aɪ] but on Martha's Vineyard,
centralization occurs as far as [əɪ] .   Similarly with /aw/
there is centralization to [əʊ] .

Table 1 (labov 1963) shows a considerable difference in
the degree of centralization of these diphthongs according to
age.   There is a noticeable peak in the 31-45 age group.

TABLE   1
CENTRALIZATION OF (ay)
AND (aw) BY AGE LEVEL

Age	(ay)	(aw)
75-	25	22
61-75	35	37
46-60	62	44
31-45	81	88
14-30	37	46

Before we can consider reasons for the differences in
centralization, some explanation is needed concerning these
figures.   We shall give on page 77 a section adapted from a

table in which Labov plots the degree of centralization for one of his informants.

TABLE 2

Grade	0	1	2		0	1	2	
right	xx	xxxx	xxxxxx		xxxx	xx	xxxx	out
night	xx	xx	x		x	x		about
white			x		x	x		trout
like		xx				x		house
sight	xxx	x			xx	x		south
(ay) - 104							(aw) - 78	

All occurrences of the two diphthongs were plotted according to the degree of centralization on a three point scale. Thus, in this section of the table there are 7 uncentralized occurrences of the /ay/ diphthong, 9 semi-centralized occurrences and 8 centralized occurrences. Giving a rating of 0, 1 and 2 respectively, we have (7 x 0) + (9 x 1) + (8 x 2) = 25. The total number of occurrences of the /ay/ diphthong is 24. Thus, this speaker would be given the value of $\frac{25}{24}$ x 100 = 104 for (ay). The same speaker has 18 occurrences of the /aw/ diphthong and scores 14 points. Thus, he would be given the value of $\frac{14}{18}$ x 100 = 78 for (aw). Naturally, these values could change if the data of the whole table were to be considered.

The high degree of centralization in the 31-45 age group appears to Labov to be related to a reaction against social change, particularly against the increase in ownership of island property by outsiders. In another table Labov shows a considerable geographical variation in centralization.

TABLE   3
GEOGRAPHICAL DISTRIBUTION
OF CENTRALIZATION

	(ay)	(aw)
Down-island	35	33
Edgartown	48	55
Oak Bluffs	33	10
Vineyard Haven	24	33
Up-island	61	66
Oak Bluffs	71	99
N. Tisbury	35	13
West Tisbury	51	51
Chillmark	100	81
Gay Head	51	81

The figures for Chillmark are particularly significant for him.
As Labov states "the only place where fishing is still a major
part of the economy, Chillmarkers are the most different,
independent, the most stubborn defenders f their way of
living."

The above is a highly simplified statement of Labov's
findings and conclusions.   The reason for the change towards
centralization seems to be that those who wish to remain on the
island have the Chillmark fishermen as a reference group and
they will copy and even exaggerate the centralization of this
conservative group.

POINTS FOR DISCUSSION

1. Labov (1963) gives as reasons for his choice
of Martha's Vineyard the fact that it is a
self-contained unit but with "enough social
and geographic complexity to provide ample
room for differentiation of linguistic
behavior."   He also mentions the fact of
the Linguistic Atlas of New England as a
background for the investigation.

What would be a suitable area for such an
investigation in your region?   How would you justify

the choice?   You might not be able to work in an
area like Martha's Vineyard, separated by a three
mile stretch of water, but a linguistic community
could be socially isolated because of social
status, ethnic background or employment

2.   Labov illustrates a scale of values from
     0 to 2 for degrees of centralization.
     (He *mentions* a four point scale but only
     illustrates a three point one).   Such a
     scale might not be appropriate for *all*
     phonic features.   Justify the choice of
     a particular scale for some phonic feature.

3.   Is Labov's explanation plausible?   In his
     presentation, Labov shows that there is much
     more centralization among teenage students
     intending to remain on the island than those
     who are not.   If you were considering rural
     area teenagers elsewhere, could one nec-
     essarily equate the degree of occurrence of
     a linguistic feature common in that area with
     the teenagers' intention to remain in the
     area or move to a big city?   What other
     factors might there be?

6.2   *Some other examples of phonic change in progress*

     Gimson (1962) gives a number of examples of change in the
RP (Received Pronunciation) variety of British English.

     When discussing RP he refers to "the *conservative* RP forms
used by the older generation and, traditionally, by certain
professions or social groups;   the *general* RP forms most
commonly in use and typified by the pronunciation adopted by
the BBC;   and the *advanced* RP forms mainly used by young
people of exclusive social groups - mostly of the upper classes,
but also, for prestige value, in certain professional circles.
In its most exaggerated variety, this last type would be
judged 'affected' by other RP speakers, in the same way that
all RP types are liable to be considered affected by those who
use unmodified regional speech.   Advanced pronunciations,
however, whenever they are not the result of temporary fashion,
may well indicate the way in which the RP system is developing
and be adopted in the future as general   RP   e.g. the
originally advanced ('affected') diphthong in *home*, involving
increased centralization and a tendency towards monophthong-
ization, seems likely to become general in a very short time."

An interesting case is the /I/ phoneme as in *hit, kill, swim*. Gimson states "a conservative RP form may be much closer than the general RP /I/ .... coming nearer to the quality associated with /i:/; other speakers, often of advanced RP use a type which is less than half-close (= $\begin{bmatrix}"\\e\\‿\end{bmatrix}$), especially in unaccented syllables." Thus we have the observation of a considerable sound change movement. Examples of the 'conservative' type may be heard from older Anglican clergy and from recordings, e.g. of politicians earlier this century. Bertrand Russell, the philosopher, had a noticeably close form in words like *discipline*.

Regarding the /ɒ/ phoneme as in: *pot, Ron, bog*, he gives a sociolinguistic explanation for a change. He mentions that "Many words containing /ɒ/ + /f, θ, s/ have an alternative pronunciation with /ɔ:/, e.g. *off, cloth, cross*. Such a variant is typical of conservative RP and has a social prestige in southern England, but is generally being replaced in the speech of the younger generation by /ɒ/. This shift away from the traditional /ɔ:/ in such contexts may be due to the fact that /ɔ:/ is also typical of popular London speech (Cockney), which uses /ɔ:/ in these situations and also in such words as *dog, gone*, etc."

In Australia, one can observe a gradual replacement of the aspirated fortis alveolar stop [t] by an unaspirated, lenis form. There is a noticeable increase in the occurrence of the lenis, unaspirated alveolar stop intervocalically in such words as *butter, better, letter* so that the distinction between *latter* and *ladder*, uttered out of context, is the greater vowel length in the first syllable of the latter word - *ladder*. There seems to be some evidence of a comparable change with /k/ but not with /p/.

POINTS FOR DISCUSSION

1. Gimson was not writing as a sociolinguist and this makes his observations of particular interest as he was not writing a work in which he wished to give a social motivation for linguistic phenomena. If you examine the changes that are in progress in RP English, can you predict whether all 'advanced' forms will become a part of general RP? Are there any inhibiting factors?

2. Gimson suggests in the case of /ɒ/ as against /ɔ:/ a movement *away from* a less socially

prestigious form. Are there circumstances in which there might be movement *towards* a less socially prestigious form? It seems that in Australia, there is a movement from a former prestige norm of RP towards a more distinctively Australian norm. Does this type of change also occur *within* a country, without relation to outside norms? What might be the social motivation for such a change?

3. Consider whether there is evidence of consonantal change in the speech area with which you are familiar.

6.3 *Changes in lexicon and syntax*

Words come into vogue, especially with some groups, and disappear quickly again. Groups of young people often have popular or 'in' words. If these words were to be put to another group in the following year, most would be rejected as dated.

However, lexical items or lexical groups may refer to new concepts or they may refer to established concepts in a new way. In such cases, there is probably a greater chance of survival. Thus terms like *autistic, socially deprived,* etc., may reflect changes in social attitudes.

Changes in syntax may also be observed. In some English speaking countries, prescriptive attitudes to such matters as avoidance of split infinitives, not ending a sentence with a preposition, careful distinction between *each other* and *one another,* and between *between* and *among* seem to be on the wane.

Another change involving syntax is the use of *hopefully* as a sentence adverbial. Some years ago, the general British and Australian usage would have restricted the use of *hopefully* to a Manner Adverbial as in: The Prime Minister spoke *hopefully* about the economic future of the country (= in a hopeful way). It is now common to hear or read such examples as (Robinson 1972:186) "In the course of the previous nine chapters we have raised many more questions than we have answered, but *hopefully* we can at least begin to see some profitable directions for further enquiry." This obviously does not mean that we can begin *in a hopeful way* but rather that *it is to be hoped that we can begin* .. Another use by the same writer (1972:29) is: "Hence we shall encounter quite a number of new words, as well as old words in new, and *hopefully* more precise, senses."

Again, hopefully is used in the sense of *it is to be hoped*.
This usage has been common in the U.S.A. for some time but is
certainly more recent in Britain and Australia.

POINTS FOR DISCUSSION

1.   Were you taught any prescriptive grammar
      rules such as 'not splitting infinitives'
      at school?   Do you observe these rules now?

2.   One might speculate that *hopefully* was first
      used as a sentence adverbial in Britain and
      Australia mainly by those who had greater
      contact with American publications, e.g. in
      sociology, education, psychology and
      linguistics.   How might one test this
      hypothesis?

3.   Are there words which were in fashion with
      your group a year or so ago but which are
      now considered old-fashioned?   You may have
      to think rather hard as your own usage pro-
      bably changed imperceptibly.

4.   Can you think of any social motivation for
      any changes which you think have occurred
      or are occurring?

6.4   *Planned Language Change*

Of course, discussion of language change and its social
motivation is closely connected to language planning policies
to be discussed in Chapter 9.   The social motivation for
changes in the language may be far more conscious than in the
cases discussed so far, and it may be that there is definite
governmental action.

ASSIGNMENTS AND EXERCISES

1.   Make a short list of lexical items (10, for
      example) which you feel you would not use
      but which older people use.   Ask people of
      your own age group:

      (a) whether they would use them;

      (b) whether they consider them old fashioned.

      Giving a 0 rating for a negative answer in each

case and 1 for a positive answer, give a
'value' for each word.   Thus, if you
asked 20 people and 14 gave a positive
answer for a particular word, the value
would be 70.

2.   Choose a structure which you feel may have
      only recently become acceptable, e.g.
      *Hopefully, there will soon be a reduction
      in the cost of living* and matching it with
      its more traditional paraphrase, *It is to
      be hoped that there will soon be a reduction
      in the cost of living,* determine which is
      preferred by a sample of members of the
      community of various ages.   The investi-
      gation could be made more comprehensive by
      also considering social and occupational
      differences.

3.   Labov gives as a reason for a linguistic
      change identification with a certain idealized
      type.   Gimson, in the case of the /ɒ/ - /ɔ:/
      distinction, gives as a possible reason for
      linguistic change the desire *not* to be identi-
      fied with speakers of a certain variety of
      English.   Of course, both forces could work
      at the same time.   By means of questionnaires
      administered to persons who seem to have moved
      in the direction of a linguistic change, try
      to find the motivation for their change.

4.   Make a 'Martha's Vineyard' type investigation
      of a sound change.   You may well have to use
      a smaller sample of speakers.   Again, this
      could be a joint investigation.

5.   By investigating copies of the same newspaper
      at intervals of say 10 years, try to find
      evidence of linguistic change.   It would be
      necessary to compare the same type of writing,
      e.g. a comparison of editorials or of
      financial reports.   You may get a hunch
      about changes in sentence structure, e.g.
      number of clauses per sentence or the fre-
      quency of longer words, e.g. over 3 syllables
      and be able to investigate this over a period
      of time.   Earlier copies of newspapers are
      usually available in larger libraries.

6.   Try to find a linguistic feature which is
      conservative in the sense that it is more
      common in the speech of older members of
      the community.   Try to find the degree
      of occurrence of this feature in the
      speech of younger members of the community.
      Is there any relationship between high
      occurrence and social attitudes?

RECOMMENDED   READING

Labov   W. 1972.   The social motivation of a sound change.
         In *Sociolinguistic patterns*.   Philadelphia : Univer-
         sity of Pennsylvania Press.

         This article was first published in 1963 in *Word*,
         19:273-309.

Saussure F. de 1962.   *Cours de linguistique générale*.
         Paris : Payot.   Chapter III gives Saussaure's views
         on the need for distinction between synchrony and
         diachrony.

         The most readily available English translation is in
         a paperback edition:
         1966.   New York : McGraw-Hill Book Company.

7.   BILINGUALISM   AND   OTHER   MULTILINGUALISM

7.0   The terms *bilingual* and *bilingualism* cover a wide range
of situations, communities and individuals.   In popular usage,
one may say that a person is bilingual (or is a bilingual) if
he speaks two languages, no matter to what degree.   The term
multilingual is less common but is appropriate when it is a
matter of more than two languages.   A country like Canada or
Belgium may be referred to as bilingual and perhaps one like
India as multilingual.

However, we shall need to consider the problems of bi- and
multilingualism in somewhat more detail, although the subject
is so vast that we can deal with only some aspects of it.

7.1   *Diglossia*

The term *diglossia* was used by Ferguson (1959) to describe
situations such as those he exemplified in the Arabic speaking
countries (e.g. Egypt, Iraq, Syria), Greece, Switzerland and
Haiti.

In these countries, Ferguson states, there is a High (H)
variety and a Low (L) one.   For example, in Haiti there is the
(H) French and the (L) créole;   in Greece there are the (H)
katharévusa and the (L) *dhimotiki*.

Ferguson claims that one of the most important features of
diglossia is the specialization of function for H and L.   He
gives a table suggesting the types of situations in which each
variety would be used:

	H	L
Sermon in church or mosque	x	
Instructions to servants, waiters, workmen, clerks		x
Personal letter	x	
Speech in parliament, political speech	x	
University lecture	x	
Conversation with family, friends, colleagues		x
News broadcast	x	
Radio 'soap opera'		x
Newspaper editorial, news story, caption on picture	x	
Caption on political cartoon		x
Poetry	x	
Folk literature		x

Speakers regard H as superior and in fact may even deny the existence of L so that an outsider would be taught only the H, even though the H form is quite inappropriate for many functions.

Usually, children learn the L variety in the home and the H variety is acquired only after schooling commences.

Ferguson's discussion of *diglossia* related purely to situations where the H and L varieties are related even if not fully mutually comprehensible. Thus a child might not understand lexical items in the H variety even though these referred to everyday objects. This is a different situation from that in, for example, English speaking countries where, although the young child would not understand lexical items like *interrelationship* or *disillusioned*, he would not have to learn at a later stage other words for *house, water, but, give, now, donkey*, to quote some examples given by Ferguson.

POINTS FOR DISCUSSION

1.   What social and/or historical conditions would most likely lead to and maintain a diglossia situation as described by Ferguson?   Ferguson discusses this but

you may get some clues from his four
examples of diglossia situations.

2.   What social and/or historical conditions
     would most likely lead to the breakdown
     of such a situation?   Ferguson offers a
     tentative prognosis for the four sit-
     uations and suggests the *least* change
     for the Swiss German situation.

3.   (i)   In what other areas does diglossia
            as described by Ferguson occur?

     (ii)   Could the term *diglossia* be
            appropriately applied to other
            situations where two more distantly
            related or even 'unrelated' lang-
            uages perform the L and H functions,
            e.g. a local language performing the
            L function and the official national
            language or the language of a past
            or present colonial administration
            performing the H function?

7.2   *Diglossia and Bilingualism*

   Fishman extends and modifies the concept of diglossia
and discusses the interrelationship of diglossia and bilingualism.   The possible relationships between the two are shown in
the matrix below (adapted from Fishman 1971b:288)

+   DIGLOSSIA   -

	1. Both diglossia and bilingualism	2. Bilingualism without diglossia
+ BILINGUALISM		
−	3. Diglossia without bilingualism	4. Neither diglossia nor bilingualism

   Fishman suggests a wider definition of diglossia as long
as the two varieties are *functionally* separated.   Thus, for
example, in Puerto Rican areas of New York City, (Puerto Rican)
Spanish would be the L and (American) English the H.
Referring to Gumperz (1961, 1962, 1964a, 1964b, 1966) he states
(1971b) that "diglossia exists not only in multilingual societ-

ies which officially recognize several 'languages', and not
only in societies that utilize vernacular and classical varieties but also in societies which employ separate dialects,
registers or *functionally differentiated varieties of whatever
kind*."

Thus one could claim that diglossia exists in regard to
the English speaking communities in countries like Britain, the
U.S.A. or Australia because very different varieties (sociolects, styles, registers) are used for different functions.
If the extension of the term *diglossia* to such a situation
seems to be inappropriate in comparison with Ferguson's cases,
one should compare an *actual* sample of educated formal speech
with an *actual* sample of 'uneducated' informal speech.   The
differences, not only in syntax and in range of lexicon, but
also in actual lexical items, could come as a surprise.

We may now consider the four combinations possible according to Fishman's diagram.   A brief and clear exemplification
and explanation of the first three types is given by Verdoodt
(1972).

7.3   *+Diglossia +Bilingualism*

Fishman suggests that there are few *nations* which are in
this category but an approximation to it would be Paraguay
where more than half of the population speaks both Spanish and
Guarani (Rubin 1962, 1967) as H and L respectively.   Other
regions below the national level mentioned by Fishman are the
Swiss-German cantons, pre-World War I Eastern Europe where
Jewish males communicated with one another in Hebrew (H) and
Yiddish (L) and the French speaking part of Canada where
English and French have (H) and (L) functions respectively in
certain interactions.   It would be an oversimplification to
class French as the L language in general in a city like
Montreal.   However, it appears (Hughes 1972) that French has
the L language function in certain business organizations and
industrial plants.

Fishman suggests (1971b) that the typical +diglossia
+bilingualism situation is one where there is "a fairly large
and complex speech community such that its members have
available to them both a range of *compartmentalized* roles as
well as ready *access* to these roles."

We feel that it would seem to be useful to make a distinction between *intragroup* and *intergroup* +diglossia +bilingual-
ism.   The former would seem to be typified by the Arabic
speaking countries where both the local variety of Arabic *and*

classical Arabic are used for communication *among* members of
the general speech community.   Intergroup +diglossia
+bilingualism would be typified by the Montreal situation where
the French speaking community would mainly use French for intra-
group communication and English for communication with non-
speakers of French.   (Although, it seems that some native
speakers of French would converse together in English on
certain specialized topics, e.g. scientific.)   The Puerto
Rican areas of New York would seem to be an intermediate system
as it would seem that bilingual Puerto Ricans use Spanish or
English according to the domain: Spanish for family and
friendship;   English for religion, work and education.
(Greenfield 1970).   In the Montreal situation, the French
speaking community would use French (and Latin) in the religious
domain, French in the educational domain and, in many cases,
French in the work domain.

7.4   +*Diglossia -Bilingualism*

     Examples of this situation could be found in many
European countries in the pre-World War I era (Fishman 1971)
where, for example, French in Russia and Rumania, German in
Hungary were the H languages and the vernacular was the L.

     Another example is given by Verdoodt (1972) in a very
clear explanation of the characteristics of diglossia and
bilingualism.   In Alsace and eastern Lorraine there is "an
upper-class speaking French (and partly coming from the French-
speaking part of the country) and a lower-class speaking a
German dialect, each with a language appropriate to its own
restricted concern."

     Of course, in such a situation, one would find some
individuals who are bilingual and who can express themselves
in both speech varieties, but basically one can distinguish two
distinct speech communities.

     Somewhat similar situations obtained in some colonial
countries with the H language being that of the colonial power
and the L language(s) being spoken by the local population.
Intergroup communication was greatly restricted but there were
some (at least partial) bilinguals.   Thus, a few of the local
population, e.g. persons in minor administrative positions,
might speak the language of the colonial power and some of the
colonial administrators might speak the local language(s).
Thus in the period before World War II, the police force in the
Malay States set examinations in Malay for British police
officers working there.

7.5   -Diglossia +Bilingualism

Here Fishman gives no actual examples of such a situation but he makes the important point (1971b) that "bilingualism is essentially a characterization of individual linguistic versatility whereas diglossia is a characterization of the social allocation of functions to different languages or varieties."

Verdoodt (1972) gives the example of East-Belgiun where "although not all persons are bilingual (those who are normally being German-French bilinguals ....) the majority is bilingual and able to express private as well as public affairs in both languages.   Nevertheless, without the benefit of a well under-stood and widely accepted social concensus as to which language is to be used between which interlocutors for communication concerning what topics or for what purposes, no diglossia pattern has been established."

7.6   -Diglossia -Bilingualism

Fishman suggests (1971b) that "only very small, isolated and undifferentiated speech communities may be said to reveal neither diglossia nor bilingualism."   However, he claims that such groups are easier to hypothesize than to find.

One might imagine an isolated Australian tribe or the population of a small Pacific island (in both cases before European contact) but even here there was often differentiation. Thus, among many Australian aboriginal tribes there were differences in male and female speech, secret languages spoken only by initiated males or 'mother-in-law languages' used when speaking (in an indirect way) to certain kin.   (Dixon 1971)

The most likely speech community to fill the bill would be an isolated group of monolinguals in the early days of an experiement in egalitarian communal living in an isolated area. However, if one restricted the concept of diglossia to Ferguson's original one, then there would be quite a number of non-diglossic, non-bilingual speech communities, e.g. many rural communities generally considered as monolingual and with-out sharp social stratification, e.g. in Australia and New Zealand.

POINTS FOR DISCUSSION

1.   We have concentrated on *bi*-lingualism and
     di-glossia.   What would be examples of
     combinations that could include *three*

or more language varieties?   Consider,
for example, communities where there could
be an H speech variety of the elite and two
L speech varieties of the mass of the people.
Or a community with an H variety, an L variety
and an R (Religious) variety, e.g. England in
the post-Norman conquest period.

2.   What is likely to happen in a +bilingual
      +diglossia situation if the government decrees
      universal education in *both* speech varieties?

3.   How would a nation like The Netherlands or
      Sweden fit in if we consider the following?
      In both countries, there is a national
      language which is used for all the purposes
      listed in Ferguson's table.   However, in
      both countries, English is the main second
      language taught in schools, is widely used
      by persons writing books and articles of a
      'learned' nature and is understood by a con-
      siderable part of the community so that they
      are, for example, able to converse fluently
      in English on many topics.

7.7   *Two Particular Cases*

We can now consider two cases which do not seem to fit
neatly into Fishman's scheme.   Of course, so much of what is
observable about language and language behaviour is on a
continuum and there would be continuous gradation within the
possibilities of + or - Diglossia, + or - Bilingualism.   Thus
one can imagine a +Diglossia -Bilingualism situation changing to
a +Diglossia +Bilingualism situation with greater access to the
H language available because of increased educational facilit-
ies.

A.   *Singapore in the 19th and early 20th Centuries*

In the 19th century, when Singapore was one of the
British Straits Settlements, English was the language of
administration and each ethnic group spoke its own language.
However, Bazaar Malay had developed for basic inter-ethnic
communication.   Thus the speech repertoire of the typical
British government official or employee with a private firm
(or his wife) would be English as main language and Bazaar
Malay as a means of communication on basic matters with Malays,
Chinese and Indians.

Most members of these other speech communities had their
own language for intra-group communication and Bazaar Malay for
inter-ethnic group communication.

Gradually, some Asians learned English and were employed
in private industry and government as clerks, teachers, etc.
Thus, their speech repertoire would be English (to a greater
or lesser degree), their own language and Bazaar Malay.

There were also some Asians who spoke a pidgin English -
mainly shopkeepers and others who came into contact with the
more transient European visitors.   For a fuller account see
Platt (1975a, 1975b).

This was a kind of situation in which most of the population was bilingual in the ethnic language and Bazaar Malay.
Certainly, Bazaar Malay was considered a low speech form but
it did not perform the typical functions of the Ls mentioned
in our previous discussion.   It was purely for inter-group
communication.

The problem is increased if we consider the English
speaking Asians.   For them, English could well have been considered the H form for domains like Employment and Education
(and for some, Church) with their ethnic language for the
Family and Friendship domains and Bazaar Malay for what we
might call the 'Transactions' domain - inter-ethnic communication in connection with shopping and transport.   In some
cases, Bazaar Malay would also have been used in the Employment
domain, e.g. by a Chinese speaking to Tamil or Malay employees
in lower positions.   For many of these Asians, English would
have been considered extremely important, but there would
still have been an awareness of their own cultural heritage,
connected with their own ethnic language.   For some, it could
have been that the ethnic language should be considered as H1,
English as H2 and Bazaar Malay as L.   Or for some perhaps
(especially those who were trying to identify with English
values) English would have been H, their own ethnic language
M(edium) and Bazaar Malay L.

B.   *Present Day Singapore*

In Singapore today, there is an official policy which is
in a sense bilingual and in a sense quadrilingual.   Radio and
television broadcasts, official announcements, etc., are in
English, Chinese (Mandarin), Malay and Tamil.   Every child
takes two languages at school.   If the first (the main
language of instruction) is English, then Mandarin, Malay or
Tamil is the second.   If Mandarin, Malay or Tamil is first,

then English will be the second.   Actually a majority of
children now take English as first language, the second biggest
group taking Mandarin as first language.

We shall concentrate on the Chinese ethnic group as the
numerically dominant one.   The typical Chinese who attends an
English medium school (or school 'stream') acquires the
parents' (particularly mother's) southern Chinese 'dialect'
(e.g. Hokkien or Cantonese) first but may acquire the local
colloquial English soon afterwards from elder siblings.   At
school, the child will be taught English and Mandarin and will
acquire greater competence in Colloquial Singapore English
(Platt 1975a, 1975b).   He or she may also informally acquire
another Chinese dialect or two from friends and/or workmates.

Thus there is a situation where the typical ethnically
Chinese Singaporean will have the following verbal repertoire:

1.   'Native' Chinese 'dialect'

2.   Other Chinese 'dialect(s)'

3.   Mandarin

4.   Colloquial Singapore English

5.   Formal Singapore English

6.   Some Bazaar Malay

It should be noted that 'English' means a distinctive
local variety of English (Singapore English - SE) which we have
divided here into two subvarieties: Formal SE and Colloquial
SE (*1) (for further discussion on this matter see Platt 1975a,
1975b).

Thus, the relationship of speech varieties with the 6
domains previously mentioned (Fishman's 5 domains plus the
'Transactions' domain) would be:

DOMAIN	SPEECH VARIETY
Family	'Native' South Chinese dialect with mother. 'Native' South Chinese dialect/colloquial SE with father. Mainly colloquial SE with siblings.
Friendship	'Native' South Chinese dialect. Other South Chinese dialects. Colloquial SE (*2)
Religion: Christian	Mainly formal SE
Buddhist, Taoist, etc.	Mainly 'native' Chinese dialect.
Education	Mainly Formal SE or Mandarin
Employment (e.g. government department, business office)	Mainly Formal SE, some Mandarin.
Transactions	Colloquial SE Southern Chinese dialects Some Bazaar Malay

POINTS FOR DISCUSSION

1. You may be familiar with the situation in another nation which was formerly a colony. What languages would be used for the various domains mentioned earlier?   Would there be *other* appropriate domains?

2. Given that more and more students take English
    as first language in Singapore, what would be
    your prognosis for the future in Singapore
    regarding domain - speech variety relation-
    ships?

3. In Australia it is (or was) generally the
    case that aborigines, besides speaking their
    own native variety, spoke other varieties.
    Sometimes these were on a continuum of
    mutual intelligibility;   sometimes a neigh-
    bouring group spoke a variety considerably
    different in syntax and lexicon but typically,
    aborigines had a passive knowledge of the
    other variety or varieties.   How does this
    situation fit into Fishman's diglossia -
    bilingualism system?

7.8   *Inter-language interference*

A fairly comprehensive and, in many parts, still valid
account of various aspects of bilingualism and the problems
connected with it is given in Weinreich's book *Languages in
contact* (1953).   He not only deals with the socio-cultural
setting of language contact but also investigates interference patterns of a phonological, grammatical and lexical
nature and their causes in a range of bilingual situations.

The study of interference patterns is not only of value
to the foreign language teacher but is also useful in
research into the speech of migrants and the design of migrant
teaching programs as these patterns may show up language
attitudes and general socio-cultural structures of the bilingual speech community.

Some interesting work on interference patterns, verbal
repertoires and domains of migrant groups in Australia has
been carried out by Clyne (1967, 1972).

7.9   *Degree of Bilingualism*

So far, we have not discussed the *degree* of bilingualism.
The degree of bilingualism could include (Fishman 1971b) the
language *medium,* i.e. whether a person uses only one of his
languages for reading and writing, *comprehension* of the
languages, *production* of the languages and the actual degree of
competence in each of his language abilities.   Thus a non-
native speaker of English migrating to a mainly English speaking country may at first speak his own language fluently and

English very poorly.   Gradually he may reach a stage in which
both his native language and his English would be considered
deviant.   On the other hand, he may keep up a high degree of
competence in his native language and develop very considerable
competence in English.

Fishman suggests a development over time in the case of
late 19th and early 20th century immigrants to the U.S.A. from
Stage 1 to Stage 4

BILINGUAL FUNCTIONING TYPE	DOMAIN OVERLAP TYPE	
	Overlapping Domains	Non-Overlapping Domains
Compound ('Interdependent' or fused)	2. Second Stage: More immigrants know more English and therefore can speak to each other either in mother tongue or in English (still mediated by the mother tongue) in several domains of behavior. Increased interference.	1. Initial Stage: The immigrant learns English via his mother tongue. English is used only in those few domains (work sphere, governmental sphere) in which mother tongue cannot be used. Minimal interference. Only a few immigrants know a little English.
Coordinate ('Independent')	3. Third Stage: The languages function independently of each other. The number of bilinguals is at its maximum. Domain overlap is at its maximum. The second generation during childhood. Stabilized interference.	4. Fourth Stage: English has displaced the mother tongue from all but the most private or restricted domains. Interference declines. In most cases both languages function independently; in others the mother tongue is mediated by English (reverse direction of Stage 1, but same type).

Type of Bilingual Functioning and Domain
Overlap During Successive Stages of Immigrant Acculturation

An example of 'stabilised interference' is given by Clyne
(1970).   He mentions various rural communities in Australia,
settled by Germans in the 19th century in which "German (often
a local blending of various East Central German or other
dialects with stabilised phonic, lexical, and syntactic interference from Australian English) was, for two or three
generations, the dominant language of community, church, and
school."

POINTS FOR DISCUSSION

1. How would you try to investigate changes in the
    degree of bilingualism in migrant groups?

2. In what domains is the native language likely
    to be retained longest in the case of migrant
    groups?   You might need to consider more
    specialized areas within domains.   For
    example, within the Family domain, it may be
    retained longer in husband-wife communication
    and even longer in 'internal' speech.

3. What social conditions would tend to maintain
    a clear +diglossia +bilingualism situation?

EXERCISES AND ASSIGNMENTS

1. Test a number of bilinguals on their
    ability to name various objects in
    their two languages.

2. If you are able to obtain newspapers
    in two or more languages from a
    particular region, compare the adver-
    tisements for the same product.   In
    what way do they differ, e.g. is there
    more appeal to 'old' values in one
    language?

3. If there is radio or television
    advertising in your country, is there
    a difference in the range of products
    advertised in the different languages?
    Again, is there a difference in the
    approach to the viewer/listener?

4. If you live in a country with migrant
    groups, e.g. Australia, Canada, try to

find out how many foreign language
newspapers there are, in what languages
they are published, whether there has
been an increase or decrease in number
of newspapers in each language over a
period of time, whether there has been
an increase or decrease in circulation
of each newspaper.

5. (i)   To what extent are public
          announcements made in several
          languages in your region or
          country - which languages
          and what kinds of announcements,
          whether in the press or on radio
          or television or notices sent
          to householders?

   (ii)   If such announcements are made
          in your region or country, how
          do they relate to the numerical
          strength of each migrant group
          whose language is used in this
          way?

   (iii) How would you explain that no
          official use is made of the
          languages of some numerically
          strong migrant groups in some
          countries?

6. If you can find a person (or persons)
   with three or more speech varieties at
   their disposal, find out by questionnaires which speech varieties they use
   for which domains.

7. Bilinguals and other multilinguals often
   have various attitudes to each language.
   (Fishman 1971b:331 discusses attitudes
   to languages.) A bilingual may feel
   his native language to be better in some
   respects but his other language(s) better
   in others, e.g. he may feel his native
   language to sound better but another
   language to be clearer. Devise a set of
   questions to test attitudes regarding
   such points as: beautiful, clear in
   expression, friendly, easy, honest, etc.,

about two or more languages and obtain
attitudes of speakers on a 3 point scale
of plus, neutral and minus.

RECOMMENDED READING

Fishman   J. A. ed.   1968.   *Readings in the sociology of
language.*   The Hague : Mouton.

Section V is on Multilingualism and Section VI is on
Language Maintenance and Language Shift.

1971.   The sociology of language: an inter-
disciplinary social science approach.   In *Advances in
the sociology of language I.*   J. A. Fishman ed.,
217-380.   The Hague : Mouton.

Discussion of bilingualism occurs in various places
in this long article but Section 3:   Some basic
sociolinguistic concepts, Section 6:   Societal bilingualism: stable and transitional, and Section 7:
Language maintenance and language shift, are
particularly important.

1972.   ed.   *Advances in the sociology of language
II.*   The Hague : Mouton.

Section III: Bilingualism and diglossia, includes
4 articles on bilingual situations and Section IV:
Language maintenance and language shift, is related
to the same broad topic.   One of the five articles
in this section is the one previously mentioned by
Verdoodt.

Pride   J. B. and Holmes J. eds.   1972.   *Sociolinguistics.*
Harmondsworth : Penguin.

Part One: Bilingualism and Multilingualism and
Part Two: Standard Language and National Language
are relevant.

Weinreich U.   (1953) 1964.   *Languages in contact.*   The
Hague : Mouton.

Footnotes

(*1)   In reality, of course, the matter is far more complex
as SE can be considered as a speech continuum with at
least 3 sub-variety clusters.

(*2)   The hierarchy of usage of the speech varieties
        mentioned depends to a great extent on the age and
        socio-economic status of the interlocutors.   For
        further discussion of the 'age variable' see
        Chapter 5.

CHAPTER 8

8.   PIDGINS,   CREOLES   AND   RELATED   PHENOMENA

8.0   *Attitudes to Pidgins and Creoles*

   Pidgins and creoles have in the past been considered
mongrel or bastard languages, not appropriate to be taught at
schools or made official languages of a region.

   The pioneer in the field of pidgin and creole studies is
generally considered to be Schuchardt who in the 19th century
wrote on pidgins and creoles spoken in various parts of the
world.

   Although some well known linguists such as Jespersen
(1922), Bloomfield (1933) and Hjelmslev (1939) recognized the
importance of pidgins and creoles, generally little attention
was paid to them by most linguists until the fifties and
sixties when there was an upsurge of interest in this type of
language.   One reason for this can be seen in the gradual
shift from a purely 'language' orientated approach to the
emergence of interest in language in social context and the
relation between linguistic and socio-economic factors.

   A name particularly associated with studies in the pidgin
and creole field and who advocated recognition of them as
languages not only worthy of study but of being national
languages of emerging nations in which they are spoken is that
of Robert A. Hall, Jr.   His *Hands off Pidgin English* (1955)
was a plea for New Guinea Pidgin to be recognized as the
official language of that country and his *Pidgin and Creole
Languages* (1966) is an easy to read introduction to the topic
although it should be pointed out that some of his views have
been challenged.

8.1   *Pidgins*

   The traditional etymology of the word 'pidgin' is as being
derived from the English 'business' but there is some disagree-
ment on this point.   The word was first applied to Chinese
pidgin English and later to similar types.

Pidgins typically have a limited vocabulary and a very reduced grammatical structure;   usually gender and number are omitted as well as many other morphological and syntactic features. They arose from a fusion of several languages (often totally unrelated) such as Chinese dialects/English, African dialects/French, African dialects/Portuguese.   This does not mean that they consist of a hotch-potch of language units thrown together.   Pidgins have their own structures and internal organization, however limited, and should be considered as speech varieties in their own right.

Many pidgins seem to have been created from a fusion of several non-European languages with at least one European language such as Portuguese, French or English but there are also other instances, e.g. the Chinook Jargon which was used mainly in trading by northwestern American Indians.

The function of a pidgin was essentially in trading situations and in employment situations, where speaker A did not speak the native language of speaker B and vice versa. The most important factor about pidgins is that there existed no speech community whose speakers had them as their primary, i.e. their native languages.

Pidgins have arisen in many situations. Some have hardly developed at all, some have lasted only very briefly, while others have shown considerable development and have had quite a long history. Some very basic pidgins, which have at times been referred to as *incipient pidgins* or *jargons,* have arisen in certain situations where speakers of different languages came into relatively brief contact, such as between explorers and the native population, or between foreign armies and the local population, etc.   There is, of course, a continuum from the completely ad hoc and ephemeral contact speech variety through to languages like New Guinea Pidgin (Neomelanesian, Tok Pisin) (see Wurm 1966, 1970, Laycock 1970, Mühlhäusler 1974) which is now in a process of creolization.

Some examples of pidgins from Hall (1966) are:

An Earlier Chinese, English-based Pidgin

télər, máj hǽv kǽći wən-pisi plɛ́nti hǽnsəm silka. máj wɔ́nci jú méki wən nájs ivniŋ drɛ́s.	Tailor, I have a very fine (piece of) silk. I want you to make a nice evening dress.

An Australian Aboriginal, English-based Pidgin

tɔ́mi, jú bɪ́n sí ðǽtwən lúbra?

Tommy, did you see that native woman?

jú síɪm lɔŋ ́áj bɪlɔ́ŋ ju?

Did you see her with your own eyes?

jɛ́s, mí bɪ́n síɪm

Yes, I saw her.

A more developed Pidgin - New Guinea Pidgin

naw mi stap rabəwl.   mi stap lɔŋ
bɪglajn, mi kətɪm kopra.   naw
wənfɛlə mastər bɪlɔŋ kəmpəni
ɛm i-kɪčɪm mi, mi kʊk lɔŋ ɛm
gɛn.

Then I stayed in Rabaul.   I was in the work-group, cutting copra.   Then a white man from the company took me as a cook again.

8.2   *Creoles*

The term creole (from Portuguese crioulo) originally meant a white man of European descent, born and raised in a tropical colony.   Later, the meaning was extended to include others of non-European or mixed origin.   (De Camp 1971a, Cassidy 1961).

Creoles are pidgins which have become primary languages, i.e. a speech community uses a creole as its first, its 'native' language of communication.   The structure of the original pidgin is expanded to enable it to fulfil its new function.   The range of lexical items is vastly increased, usually from one of the source languages or by compounding and/or reduplication, and new syntactic-semantic concepts develop.

The table below, adapted from Stewart (1968) uses four features to define different language types.   The features are:

1.   *Standardization* "i.e. the codification and acceptance, within a community of users, of a formal set of norms defining 'correct' usage."

2.   *Autonomy* "i.e. the function of the linguistic system as a unique and independent one."

3.   *Historicity* "i.e. the linguistic system is known or believed to be the result of normal development over time."

4.   *Vitality* "i.e. use of the linguistic system by an
     unisolated community of native speakers."

1	2	3	4	Type
+	+	+	+	Standard
-	-	+	+	Dialect
-	-	-	+	Creole
-	-	-	-	Pidgin

It can be seen that creoles differ from pidgins by possessing
feature 4, namely 'Vitality', the use of the linguistic system
by an unisolated community of native speakers.

According to De Camp (1971a) creoles are spoken today by
more than six million persons in and around the Caribbean and
by smaller groups in West Africa, South Africa and in South and
South-East Asia.

Creoles are usually classed according to the source
language with which they share most of their lexical items,
e.g. there are English-based creoles, Portuguese-based creoles,
French-based creoles and even Swahili-based creoles (Polomé
1968).   For research into various creoles in different parts
of the world, see the special section of the reading list at
the end of this chapter.

POINTS FOR DISCUSSION

1.   Consider other actual cases where some sort
     of contact language, however brief its life,
     would have arisen.   Why would some of these
     endure and even develop while others disappear?

2.   In Singapore and Malaya before the Japanese
     occupation, Bazaar Malay, a pidginized form
     of Malay, was the common inter-ethnic means
     of communication.   Why was this used rather
     than a pidgin English when the area was under
     British rule (in the case of Singapore and
     the other Straits Settlements) or British
     protection?

3.   Under what conditions would a speech variety
      remain and develop for a long time as a
      pidgin without becoming a creole?

4.   If a creole were accepted as the national
      language of a nation, what might be some
      problems in regard to an orthography?
      would it be better to base the orthography
      on that of the related European language,
      e.g. French, English, or devise a straight-
      forward orthography (possibly phonemic)
      based purely on the creole itself?   What
      points could be made either way?

5.   Why would it be difficult for an outsider
      eager to learn a creole to obtain instruction
      in it?

8.3   *Polygenetic versus Monogenetic Theories*

Regarding the origin of European-based pidgins, there has
arisen a controversy between a *monogenetic* theory which postulates a common 'generic' ancestor for all European-based
pidgins and a *polygenetic* theory according to which each
pidgin would be the result of a unique creation and development.
De Camp (1971a) gives a good presentation of the opposing views.

As many factors have been advanced for and against both
theories it may be advisable to present some of the more
important arguments in tabulated form.   The sequence chosen
here should not be taken as a hierarchy of importance.

Pro-Monogenetic/ Against Polygenetic	Pro-Polygenetic/ Against Monogenetic
1. Typological similarities between French-, English-Spanish-based creoles, etc., are too great for coincidence (e.g. some common vocabulary and ways of structuring). 2. All European based pidgins (and creoles) are *relexifications* of an earlier Portuguese-based pidgin used as a trade jargon during the slave trade. (Relexification means that when this pidgin was brought to another area, the lexicon was replaced.)	1. Very sketchy historical documentation for monogenetic argument. 2. Far Eastern Pidgin English lacks many of the features shared by other pidgins and creoles. 3. Certain pidgins and creoles developed without direct Portuguese influence: *non-English* based pidgins, e.g. Sango of the Central African Republic and Chinook Jargon. Some of the *European-based pidgins*, e.g. Amerindian pidgin English, Pitcairnese, of English-Polynesian origin, Roper River Pidgin of Australian Aboriginal-English origin.

8.4   *A 'Universals' Hypothesis for Creoles*

Bickerton (1974), basing his arguments on several creoles (including Hawaiian creole), states that creoles typically are closer in various ways to linguistic universals. As far as universals are concerned, it is his opinion "that the only universals likely to be of more than trivial interest are those which reflect specific properties of the human brain."

He suggests that pidgins, at least in their early stages, are blends of two or more languages and that a creole arises in the next generation of this mixed community, e.g. one of the plantation type. The child hears around him the various languages of the previous generation but has little access to the language of the dominant class, e.g. English or French. The pidgin spoken by the previous generation is the only speech variety really available to him. Because of the inadequacy of

the pidgin, the child - and his generation - develop it
because of their tacit knowledge of linguistic universals in
the sense discussed by Chomsky (1965).

Thus, a creole arises as the native language of the first
native born generation in a plantation or slave situation
where people from various language backgrounds have been
brought together but without the benefit of formal education
in any language.

DISCUSSION

This is a grossly simplified account of
Bickerton's hypothesis but it has been included
to illustrate a different viewpoint.   Does it
seem a likely hypothesis?

8.5   *Post-Creole Situations*

In certain cases, a creole may develop into a stage
referred to as 'post-creole'.   De Camp (1971b) suggests some
of the conditions which must be present:

1.   "The dominant official language of the community must
be the standard language corresponding to the creole."

2.   "The formerly rigid social stratification must have
partially (not completely) broken down, i.e. there must be
sufficient mobility to motivate large numbers of creole
speakers to modify their speech in the direction of the
standard, and there must be a sufficient program of education
and other acculturative activities to exert effective pressures
from the standard language on the creole."

These pressures affect various creole speakers to varying
degrees so that the effect obtained is that the members of the
speech community may be ranged along a linguistic continuum.
The upper part of such continuums is usually referred to as
acrolect (the 'standard', usually close to the European source
language but exhibiting in some cases local distinctive qual-
ities).   The lowest part is usually referred to as the
basilect (creole or a near-creole variety).   If clustering
occurs somewhere between the two extremes and one can identify
intermediate speech varieties, these would be termed *mesolects*.
Whether or not there is 'intermediate clustering' depends
largely on the type of the speech continuum.

Post-creole continuums, such as the one found in Jamaica,

developing from an English-based creole, provide particularly
interesting fields of study for the sociolinguist.

In order to place speakers on a linguistic continuum, one
needs to establish certain distinctive features (phonological,
lexical or syntactic) which have been found to vary in the
speech of many members of the speech community. Speakers are
then ordered according to whether they possess or do not
possess these features. Below is an illustration of how
De Camp (1971b) arranged some speakers of the Jamaican speech
community according to the absence or presence of certain
features.

Step One: Certain features were chosen, as shown in the table
below.

Features		Speakers
+A child	-A pikni	1. +A +B +C -D +E +F
+B eat	-B nyam	2. -A +B -C -D +E +F
+C /θ~t/	-C /t/	3. -A +B -C -D -E -F
+D /ð~d/	-D /d/	4. -A -B -C -D -E -F
+E granny	-E nana	5. +A +B +C +D +E +F
+F didn't	-F no ben	6. +A +B -C -D +E +F
		7. -A +B -C -D +E -F

The feature +A indicates habitual use of the word *child*,
-A indicates the use of *pikni* or *pikini* in equivalent contexts.
Feature +D means that the speaker contrasts /ð-d/ in such pairs
as *then/den*.   Speakers were then ordered as to their usage in
one feature at a time thus:

Step Two:

+A	-A
1, 5, 6	2, 3, 4, 7

Step Three:

+A	-A	+B	-B
1, 5, 6	2, 3, 7		4

Step Four:

+C	−C	+A	−A	+B	−B
1, 5	6		2, 3, 7		4

etc.

Final Step:

+D	−D +C	−C +A	−A +F	−F +E	−E +B	−B
5	1	6	2	7	3	4

The seven speakers have now been arranged along a continuum with speaker 5 at the top end and speaker 4 at the bottom. The use of a particular +feature implies the use of all +features *to the right* on the scale. Thus, speaker 2 who uses +F (didn't) would also use +E (granny) and +B (eat) but he would not normally use +A (child).

After having established a linguistic spectrum on the basis of these linguistic variables, De Camp (1971b) then adds the socio-economic data for each speaker. A noticeable correlation can be seen between these factors, e.g. speaker 5 is a young and well educated proprietor of a successful radio and applicance shop in Montego Bay whereas speaker 4 is an elderly and illiterate peasant farmer in an isolated mountain village.

The type of scaling technique used by De Camp is a useful device for comparing actual speech performance with social status, age, sex, educational background, etc. A clear discussion of scaling and of the technique of showing the frequency of variants is given by Fasold (1970).

It has been suggested that 'Black English', the non-standard English variety spoken by many negroes in the United States, is a post-creole. Many investigations of characteristics of the continuum between the basilectal variety of this and 'standard' American English have been carried out. Results of such work are reported in Dillard (1972), Fasold (1969), Labov (1969, 1972), and Wolfram (1969, 1974).

POINTS FOR DISCUSSION

1.   What would be the advantage of ordering speakers
      first according to linguistic criteria and
      then showing the relationship between the
      speakers' positions on a speech continuum and
      certain socio-economic factors?   Would it be
      preferable to group informants first according
      to their socio-economic characteristics?
      Why?   Why not?

2.   If you are familiar with or have read about
      Black English, discuss whether or not it could
      be considered a post-creole.

8.6   *The concept of the 'Creoloid'*

There are some speech varieties which have similarities to
post-creoles but differ from them in various aspects, the most
important being that they are not derived from a pidgin.

The term 'creoloid' has been suggested by Platt (1975a,
1975b) for this type of speech variety.   He gives the
definition of a creoloid as follows:

1.   It has similar structural variables to post-creoles based
on the same language.

2.   It did not develop from a pidgin but by some other process.

3.   It developed from the transference of features into the
'standard' language from the languages of *several* (sometimes
unrelated) ethnic groups.

4.   The superordinate language is usually only *one* of the
official languages.

5.   It is used as *one* of several 'native' languages by the
speech community.

6.   It is usually also used as a lingua franca in inter-
ethnic group communication within the speech community where it
is one of the sub-varieties.

An example of a 'creoloid' is Colloquial Singapore English
(CSE).

Although a type of pidgin English was used in Singapore in

earlier days and is still today by some older people, the most widely used pidgin form has been (and still is) Bazaar Malay. SCE did not grow out of the English pidgin variety.   Its existence can be traced to the transference of certain features from the languages of local ethnic groups (mainly Chinese, but also Malay and Indian) to the English acquired by school child- ren in the English medium primary and secondary schools. These transferred features were then reinforced by the use of this variety in informal situations at school and at home among siblings (Platt 1975a, 1975b) and later in employment situa- tions.

This variety never had a pidgin type structure, i.e. drastically reduced lexicon or syntax.   SCE's semantax is flexible enough for it to be used for detailed discussions on many topics.   Yet, it is often incomprehensible to outsiders because of its structure, certain lexical items and its very distinctive phonological features (including intonation).

DISCUSSION

Discuss whether or not 'creoloid' is a useful concept.   Can you think of other examples of this type of speech variety?

EXERCISES

1.   Apply the scaling technique discussed in this chapter to present some of the data you may have found for exercises or assignments in the previous chapters.

2.   Refer to works on several creoles and compare one or several of the following linguistic features:

(a)   pronouns;

(b)   comparison of adjectives;

(c)   occurrence or non-occurrence of a copula-type verb with:

(i)   Predicate Adjective, e.g. He (is) stupid.

(ii)   Locative, e.g. He (is) in the house.

(iii) Predicate Nominals, e.g. He (is) a teacher.

(d)   aspect and tense systems.

ASSIGNMENTS

Individual ·

1.   Try to obtain information about one or more
      countries in which a pidgin or creole is
      widely spoken regarding the policies of the
      government or other organizations (e.g. missions)
      on the teaching of the pidgin or creole.

2.   Try to simplify a short text.   Imagine you had
      to explain the contents to a person having
      little competence in English.

Group

      Compare the individual results obtained in
Assignment 2 above.   Do they show many similarities
in simplification?

RECOMMENDED READING

Hall R. A. Jr. 1966.   *Pidgin and creole languages.*
      Ithaca : Cornell University Press.

      An easy to read introduction to the subject.   As
      mentioned earlier, it must be kept in mind that some of
      his views have since been challenged.

Hymes D. ed. 1971.   *Pidginization and creolization of
      languages.*   London : Cambridge University Press.

      Probably the most comprehensive book in the field, it
      contains a number of useful articles on individual
      pidgins and creoles as well as a good introduction by
      David De Camp and a survey by Ian Hancock of the pidgins
      and creoles of the world (including a map showing their
      locations).

*Some works on pidgins, creoles and post-creole stages in
various regions of the world.*

A.   *French-based*

      Haiti (Valdman 1967, 1971, d'Ans 1968)
      Martinique (Lefebvre 1974)

B. *Spanish-based*

Phillipines (Whinnom 1956, Frake 1968)

C. *English-based*

Jamaica (Le Page & De Camp 1960, Cassidy & Le Page 1967,
B. Bailey 1966, Cassidy 1971, De Camp 1971)
Guyana (Bickerton 1973)
Surinam (Sranan) (Voorhoeve 1962, 1971)
Sierra Leone (Krio) (Jones 1970)
New Guinea (Neomelanesian/New Guinea Pidgin) (Wurm 1966,
                                                          1970,
Laycock 1970, Mühlhäusler 1974)
Hawaii (Reinecke 1969, Tsuzaki 1971, Day 1973)
Pitcairn Island (Pitcairnese) (Ross & Moverley 1964)

D. *Non-European-based*

African (Sango) (Samarin 1967, 1971)
Papua (Police Motu) (Wurm 1964)
Chinook Jargon (Silverstein 1972)

9.   LANGUAGE   PLANNING   AND   OTHER   LANGUAGE   TREATMENT

9.1   *Language Planning as a Type of Language Treatment*

It seems useful to use the term *language treatment* as the more general term and to consider *language planning* as one of the types of *language treatment* (Neustupný 1970, Rubin 1973, Jernudd 1973).

Thus language treatment covers all aspects of how language is consciously treated, whether by government appointed language planning bodies, by large corporations or by a small firm whose manager decrees a new style for business letters sent out by that firm.

Language planning concerns that sub-group of language treatment usually carried out at the national level by a government appointed body.   However, as we shall see, there is, as in so many areas of sociolinguistics, a continuum from the official government sponsored planning through to localized language treatment.

9.2   *Language Choice and Intra-language Treatment*

Looked at another way, language treatment, and therefore language planning, may be divided into the areas of *language choice* and *intra-language activities*.   Here, the distinction is clearer but, hypothetically at least, the problems of planning *within* languages could affect the choice of languages. Example: In a nation, the choice has to be made whether to raise language A, B or C to the status of national language. The phonology of language B is considered more suitable for the incorporation of 'Western' technical and scientific terms. Therefore B may be chosen.

The choice of language B would most likely affect intra-language planning with respect to B.   Among other processes, its lexicon would be enlarged by the inclusion of technical and scientific terms.

9.3   *Four areas of language treatment*

The areas of language treatment may be divided as in the matrix below:

Language Treatment

```
┌─────────────────────────────────────────┐
│                                          │
│      (A)  OTHER LANGUAGE TREATMENT       │       ↑
│                                          │    more unofficial
│      ------------------------            │    and individual
│      ------------------------            │
│      ------------------------    ═       │
│  ─   ------------------------    ᵍ       │
│  ᵉ   ------------------------    ᵃ       │
│  ᵍ   ------------------------    ᵘ       │
│  ᵃ   ------------------------    ᵍ       │
│  ᵘ   ------------------------    ᵃ       │
│  ᵍ   ------------------------    ᴸ       │    more official
│  ⁿ                               │       │    and national
│  ᵃ                               │       │
│  ᴸ   (B)  LANGUAGE PLANNING      │       │
│  ᴵ       (Official Government Policy)    │       ↓
└─────────────────────────────────────────┘
```

We shall discuss the various aspects of language treatment under the four combinatorial possibilities in the following order: AI, BI, AII, BII.

AI.   *Language Treatment other than Language Planning: Which Language(s)?*

At the individual end of the continuum, there is the choice by a person whether or not to learn a language, of his own or of another nation for example, which would be useful to him in employment.

At a less individual level, there are policy decisions by companies and government departments (at the departmental level) about language requirements regarding employees.   Are they to be required to show proficiency in another language because they will be sent overseas or will they have to deal with speakers of other languages, for example?   Or in a multilingual community, will employees be required to have or attain competence in a language other than their own?   Or will they be required to have competence in the particular language which that company or government department lays down as compulsory?

For example, a British owned company in a colony in the
pre-war era would have required a certain competence in
English for its locally recruited office personnel. The diplomatic service may require future diplomatic staff to have
reached certain levels in university study of *any* language.

A level which may actually be one at which governmental
decisions may be made but which is not a matter of language
planning in the sense we are taking it is foreign language
teaching policy - which languages are to be taught? Thus, the
traditional school languages - Classical languages, French and
possibly German may be supplemented by or replaced by languages
important for trade, diplomatic relations, etc., or by the
languages of large migrant groups, e.g. (in various parts of
the world) Spanish, Russian, Japanese, Indonesian, Italian,
Modern Greek. Of course, these decisions may not necessarily
be initiated by governments (whether national or regional).
It sometimes comes about that there is pressure and possibly
financial help from business or the ethnic group(s) concerned.
This has happened in Australia where businesses have encouraged
the study of Japanese and Indonesian, and ethnic groups have
pressed for their languages to be available as school and
university subjects.

At the actual governmental level are cases of definite
government decisions (and lack of government decisions) which
are hardly worthy of being called language *planning* although
they are a type of language *treatment*. We shall call these
action and *non-action*.

1.   *Action*

Examples include: the suppression of Gaelic in Scotland
by the British after the rebellion of 1745, the attempted
imposition of German as the universal language of the Austrian
Empire by Joseph II and the later suppression of languages other
than Magyar in the Hungarian dominated region of the Austro-
Hungarian Empire in the late 19th and early 20th centuries,
although 48 percent of the population were non-Magyar.   (The
latter examples from Inglehart and Woodward 1972).

2.   *Non-Action*

In the case of a country where there may be a socially
dominant majority group speaking language A and an economically
disadvantaged minority group speaking language B, if the
government did not financially assist in the training of
teachers, then most teachers would come from group A and few

from group B.   This could affect the teaching in schools of
language B, even if the government had the attitude that language B might be taught if teachers were available.

Of course, 'lack of implementation' of a national language
policy *at a particular time* need not be considered as non-
action.   It could be a considered part of a *plan* that it would
be best to 'wait and see' for a few years after the gaining of
independence by a nation.   Thus, in a few years, antagonism to
the former colonial language might have lessened and even been
replaced by a realization that the colonial language is
important for international purposes.

Again, our example mentioned under 2. *could* be part of
carefully organized *action* to suppress a minority but it could
well be a laissez-faire attitude on the part of a government
unaware of the attitudes and aspirations of the minority group.
This may well have been so in the case of various empires, for
example in the Austrian Empire in periods when actual repress-
ive action was not taken.

3.   *Non-Action* ⟶ *Action*

This occurred recently in Australia regarding the teaching
of aboriginal children in their own languages.   Previously, a
few missions taught children literacy and basic subjects in
their own language, e.g. the Presbyterian Mission at Ernabella
in the north west of South Australia.   There were also a few
government operated schools, e.g. at Musgrave Park and Yalata
in South Australia under the authority of the South Australian
state government.   However, many mission schools and government operated schools used only English.

The use of English could be considered as *action* in some
cases but often it was really non-action as the teaching of
English stemmed from laissez-faire attitudes that the
aboriginal languages were inferior and dying out in any case,
that aborigines did not need literacy in their own languages
and that teaching them English was the natural thing.   Thus
there was a lack of action to implement the teaching of
aborigines in aboriginal languages.

In the last few years, literacy in the aboriginal languages
as well as in English has been the policy of the Australian
Commonwealth Government and there has been implementation of
this in the area under its direct control, namely the Northern
Territory.

Thus, in this instance, one can even see a change from non-action language treatment to a type of action which one can consider as language planning.

POINTS FOR DISCUSSION

1. What languages are taught in your region
    (state, province, country, etc.)?   Are
    these languages taught because of community
    demands, government decrees, or for any
    other reason?

2. If a national government took no action about
    a decision on the choice of a national lang-
    uage, what factors might lead to some
    language(s) becoming de facto the national
    language(s)?

3. Inglehart and Woodward (1972) state that in
    the Hungarian part of the Austro-Hungarian
    Empire in 1907, the Railway Servants Act
    decreed that all railway workers not con-
    versant in Magyar be fired from their jobs.
    Similar actions have probably taken place
    at other times and in other places.   In
    what ways could they have been justified
    by those who ordered them?   Are objections
    to such actions really valid *as such* or are
    they part of ethnic and/or language identity
    attitudes?

BI. *Language Planning - Which Language(s)?*

We shall consider language planning in similar terms to Jernudd and Das Gupta: "(We define language planning) as a political and administrative activity for solving language problems."   (Jernudd 1973 referring to Jernudd and Das Gupta 1971).   Basically, the government instructs a group of experts to prepare a plan.   Ideally, the experts take note of existing resources and make forecasts.   They work out a plan of action which is then approved by the government and implemented by organizations which work under the instruction of the planners. This, of course, would be an idealized example.

In reality, of course, practice falls, in varying degrees, short of the ideal.   It was suggested in the previous section that an authoritarian type of action was hardly to be considered as language planning.   However, it was suggested that there is

a continuum from the most micro-level and unplanned language
treatment to the optimum type of language planning.

If a government recognizes that there *is* a problem, then
it may deal with it and authorize language planning.   An
example nearer the optimum end of the continuum is reported by
Parker (1973) regarding Peru.   Until 1971 there had been a
uniform educational policy with Spanish the obligatory language.
At the census of 1961, the population consisted of 60 percent
monolinguals in Spanish, nearly 20 percent monolinguals in
various Indian languages, and almost 19 percent bilinguals in
Spanish and Indian languages.   The main Indian languages are
those of the Quechua family spoken mainly in the Andean region.

In January, 1972, the Ministry of Education sponsored a
National Seminar on Bilingual Education which was attended by
local and foreign experts.   The Seminar recommended that
Spanish was the only practicable candidate as a common language
for Peru but that *all* native languages should have official
status and, where appropriate, education should begin in the
local language with Spanish taught as second language.
Universities were to emphasize the study of native languages
and to train teachers and prepare teaching materials in them.

In February of the same year, the government published a
preliminary version of the educational reform law so that
public debate could take place and leading linguists of Peru
were invited to confer with the government.   Late in March,
the final version of the new law was published.

With about 80 percent of the population able to speak (at
least some) Spanish either as monolinguals or bilinguals, the
proposed reforms showed an enlightened attitude to the problem
of multilingualism.

Another case of sensible language planning is Singapore
(Platt 1975a, 1975b).   Under the colonial administration,
there was a rather piecemeal set-up.   There was free elementary
education in Malay for Malay children.   There were schools run
by Chinese and Indian community groups or private concerns
which taught in Chinese and the Southern Indian language Tamil.
There were church run and government run 'English' schools at
which the medium of instruction was English and at which fees
were charged.

The population of Singapore is now over 2 million.   The
biggest group is the Chinese, about 75 percent.   The Malays
form about 15 percent and Indians about 7 percent, with less
than 2 percent consisting of Eurasians, Europeans and other

small groups.

In 1956, an all-party parliamentary committee recommended bilingual education for Singapore and that has been the policy followed.   The importance of English for a small nation like Singapore was realized and every child takes English as first or second language.   The other three languages available are: Malay, Chinese (Mandarin) and Tamil.   If English is taken as first language, one of the others is taken as second language. If one of the others is taken as first language, English is taken as second language.   Figures for enrolment in primary and secondary schools together in 1972, according to *first* language are:

Tamil	1,278	(0.25%)
Malay	20,946	(4.08%)
Chinese	158,649	(30.88%)
English	332,878	(64.79%)

There is free choice as regards first language and second language as long as one of them is English, but the students' choice of English as first language has increased steadily.

The main problems that might be seen in this situation are:

(a)   Tamil is not the *only* language of the ethnically Indian community.   However, most Singapore Indians speak a Dravidian language and of these, Tamil is the most used. It appears that most people of Indian or Pakistani background send their children to English medium schools. The Dravidians mostly take Tamil as second language; the non-Dravidians take Malay.

(b)   Mandarin is the mother tongue of hardly any Singapore Chinese.   However, a system of separate schools or classes for Hokkien, Cantonese, Teochew, Hakka, etc., would be both expensive and divisive.   Mandarin is the national language of The People's Republic of China and of the Republic of China (Taiwan).

The language policy of Singapore appears therefore to be the most reasonable possible in such a multilingual community.

An example which might at first not seem to qualify for the designation of language planning is the case of Kenya, discussed by Gorman (1973).   In Kenya, English was 'inherited'

from the colonial power and became the language of the bureau-
cracy.   Kenya is a nation of many speech varieties.   Choosing
one of these would seem to favour one group as against the
others, but to choose English would seem to favour those with
education in English and, in any case, it would hardly be a
symbol of nationhood for an African state.

Swahili, which is widely spoken, even if not fluently in
Kenya would seem perhaps to fill the bill as it is neutral as
regards language groups in Kenya.

Some years ago, the Governing Council of KANU, the ruling
party, passed a resolution that "Swahili as our national
language shall be encouraged and enforced by all means and at
all places in Kenya and that Swahili be used in our National
Assembly."   Then in April, 1970, the party announced plans for
the extension of the use of Swahili as an official language by
stages.

According to Gorman's account, it seems that at the time
of writing, this was not a matter of *laws* but could be seen as
"a political act which had the primary objective of conveying
to Kenyans, perhaps for the first time, a sense of the importance of the language in the 'life' of the nation."   Gorman
suggests that according to the criteria of Jernudd and Das
Gupta, the scheme could be thought seriously deficient as it
made no mention of financial and human resources required for
implementation nor of the agencies to be responsible for its
implementation, evaluation and so on.   However, he suggests
that it is difficult for outsiders to judge such actions in
terms of their own criteria.

We have not touched on what is perhaps the most widely
mentioned example of language planning, concerning both which
language(s) and intra-language planning, that of Norway.
This is dealt with by Haugen (1968).   Other examples of
language planning are dealt with in articles in the works
mentioned under Recommended Reading at the end of this chapter.

POINTS FOR DISCUSSION

1.   Is language planning in the sense of 'which
      language(s)?' relevant for the United Kingdom,
      Spain, the U.S.A., The Phillipines?   You could
      add to the list.

2.   Some factors in planning a national language
      policy for a nation could include: Which

languages are spoken in the nation? What proportion of the population speaks each language as first language? What proportion of the population can speak each language? What other factors ought to be taken into consideration?

3. What factors *external* to the nation itself might legitimately be taken into consideration in formulating a language planning policy?

4. What factors other than those mentioned previously could lead to the adoption of a language which is not the native language of most of the population as national language?

5. Every nation should have only *one* national language. Is this true?

AII. *Language Treatment - Intra-Language*

Language treatment and proposals for language treatment are probably more common *within* a language than they are concerning *which* language.

In English speaking countries like the United Kingdom, the U.S.A. and Australia there is a certain amount of very low level language treatment. For example, advertisers may introduce supposedly simplified spelling, e.g. *nite* for *night, While U Wait* for *While You Wait, Rite-Way* for *Right Way.* Most of these changes are not based on any linguistic principles at all, but some do catch on and are adopted by the public, e.g. *nite.*

Writers such as popular novelists may have a certain effect on the language they use. It is possible that their syntactic structures and spelling may have some regional or national effect. Certainly, idiosyncracies of popular radio and television personalities do have an effect and their pronunciation, ways of greeting and 'pet phrases' are consciously or unconsciously adopted by many.

Business firms quite often undertake a type of language treatment by prescribing certain letter writing styles, particularly in the matter of the opening and ending, e.g. a change from Dear Sir/Madam to Dear Mr./Mrs./Miss/Ms Brown; a change from Yours faithfully to Yours cordially, etc.

The public often has views on changes or projected changes. When recently in a move towards a spelling reform, it was

suggested by some educationalists that *e* be used to represent
'the short e sound' as in *bet, said, steady,* etc., Letters to
the Editor, both for and against the proposal appeared daily
for quite some time in the newspapers.   Much of the correspondence revealed little knowledge of the problems of spelling
reform.   Many writers were simply against change;   others
were sure that this was a simplification.   Some did, justi-
fiably, point out that it was not a matter for one English
speaking country alone.   Variations in pronunciation in
different dialects of English could mean different spellings.
Thus, for those dialects which pronounce *ate* to rhyme with *met,*
the spelling would be *et,* but for dialects like Australian
English in which it rhymes with *late,* this would not be an
appropriate spelling.   For Australia and Britain, *leisure*
would presumably become *lesure* but not for the U.S.A.

English spelling is notoriously difficult but ad hoc
spelling reforms not based on a thorough knowledge of the
relationships between English phonology and morphology would
be worse than useless.   As an example, even the change from
ou to *o,* general in the U.S.A. and quite widely used in
Australia is not necessarily an improvement for all varieties
of English.   Our discussion will be exemplified from 'r-less'
dialects:

or represents $[\bar{ɔː}]$ in words like *or, port, cork.*

or represents $[\bar{ə}]$ in words like *actor, conductor, inspector*
where *-or* is an affix (e.g. *act-or,* one who acts).

our represents $[aʊ\bar{ə}]$ in words like *our, flour* (and the *ou*
segment represents $[a\bar{ʊ}]$ in words like *out, about).*

our represents $[\bar{ə}]$ in words like *favour, colour, humour*
where there is no morpheme boundary immediately before *-our.*
Note that *labour* changes to *laborious* where the pronunciation changes to $[\bar{ɔː}]$.

Thus the change from *labour* to *labor,* etc., loses a certain
regularity in sound-spelling relationship.   Of course, it
could be argued that this is a small price to pay for other
benefits but the other benefits would need to be shown.

This is *not* an argument against spelling reform.   It *is*
an argument for careful planning by experts if planning is to
take place.

Other examples of unofficial language treatment at a
national (or international) level include dictionaries such as
the Oxford and Webster series which are not official government
publications and not authorized by a government but which have
considerable prestige and are considered authoritative.
Similarly Fowler's *Modern English Usage* and similar works are
referred to and considered as appropriate arbitrators in discussions about 'correct' usage.   At a somewhat lower level are
works on letter writing, business correspondence, etc.

Our examples serve to show that there is wide interest in
language treatment and that there is a considerable amount of
language treatment at various levels of formality and various
degrees of 'spread' in regard to the part of the population
affected.

POINTS FOR DISCUSSION

1.   If it were suggested that all words having
     the sound $[ae]$ should be spelt with the
     letters *æ* so that *cat* would become *caet*
     (or perhaps *kaet*), *slap* would be *slaep*, what
     objections might be raised?   Consider pro-
     nunciations in several English-speaking
     countries.

2   There are books which lay down the 'proper'
     use of stops in abbreviations, e.g. GPO or
     G.P.O. for General Post Office, St or St.
     for Street (and Saint), Lat or Lat. for
     Latin, etc.   Do the rules laid down seem
     to be useful?

3.   Would there be value in standardizing the
     spelling of names, e.g. *Ann* and *Anne,*
     Stewart and *Stuart* could have only one
     spelling for each?   Can you think of any
     'logical' (as against the obvious emotional)
     reasons against this, particularly with sur-
     names and place names?

4.   Are certain pronunciations taught in the
     schools of your area but *not* generally used,
     e.g. is it stressed that the final sound
     of *working* is $[\eta]$ and not $[n]$?   How much
     effect does such teaching have?

5.   What about grammar and lexicon in this respect?

Are children told to avoid split infinitives,
not to use constructions such as 'It was
that big' (as against 'It was as big as *that*')?
How much effect does such teaching seem to
have?

6.   Should students at secondary and tertiary level
be corrected about 'wrong' spelling or should
they perhaps be corrected only when the 'wrong
spelling' leads to similar spelling of a homo-
phone, e.g. The trees were *bear?*

BII.   *Language Planning - Intra-language*

Alisjahbana (1971) sensibly points out that "we should
only speak of language planning in a very limited sense and for
a very special goal.   Nobody should think of planning for all
the language behavior of all the members of a nation.   Such
rigid regimentation would also mean the end of man as a think-
ing and free being."   He goes on to state that it is school-
language that lends itself to planning and regulation.
Planners can control the kinds of textbooks and teacher training.   He suggests that 'standard languages' like English,
French and German are mainly the products of compulsory
education.

It is obvious that in a new nation like Indonesia, for
which Bahasa Indonesia, based on Malay, (not on Bazaar Malay as
has often been erroneously stated), was chosen as national
language, a certain amount of prescriptivism is necessary,
especially as there were widely differing varieties in different parts of the nation in regard to affixation, lexicon and
pronunciation.   The problem for any nation embarking on a
program of planning for its national language(s) would be how
to standardize without appearing unduly prescriptive.   In the
long run, of course, no matter how prescriptive the authorities
might be, sociolectal, dialectal and various stylistic differences would arise.

In this section, instead of dealing separately with
different languages, we shall look at areas of language planning which would need to be dealt with in almost any language
planning situation.

(a)   *Phonology*

If there is a need to standardize a language which has
many regional varieties with widely differing pronunciations,

then it would be necessary to choose one particular variety as
the national standard.   Otherwise there could be problems in
producing an alphabetic orthography for the language.

(b)   *Orthography*

It is unlikely at the present time that language planning
will need to be concerned with provision of an orthography for
the first time for a national language, but orthographies may
need to be provided for minority languages.

Sometimes the problem is the provision of a new type
orthography, e.g. Roman letters to replace Arabic script.   A
well known case is that of Turkey which is mentioned by
Gallagher (1971) in a treatment of language reform there.

Often it is a matter of spelling reform as reported by
Haugen in his discussion of Norway.   The case of Malaysia and
Indonesia is interesting.   The 'Dutch' system of spelling for
Malay (Indonesian) differed considerably from the 'British'
system of romanization, e.g. *pentjoeri* (Dutch system);
penchuri (British system) for 'thief'.   In Malaya, Arabic
script was widely used but gradually, particularly after the
war, the 'British' system of romanization was adopted more and
more.

In Indonesia, there were some spelling reforms;   notably
oe was replaced by *u,* so that 'thief' was now spelt *pentjuri*.
Recently, Malaysia and Indonesia have agreed on a common
spelling reform so that this word is now *pencuri*.

(c)   *Morphology*

Asmah Haji Omar (1971) mentions that in certain colloquial
regional varieties of Malay, the verb prefixes are not used.
Thus, from the stem *timba* 'to draw water with a pail' we find
Dia menimba ayer as the formal version of 'He/She draws water
with a pail' and *Dia timba ayer* or *Dia nimba ayer* as informal
varieties.   Should the formal variety be taught or would it be
better and simpler to teach one of the informal ones?

(d)   *Syntax*

This is an area in which the problems of language planning
are particularly difficult.   The problems include which
syntactic structures to teach and which not to teach in schools
and also whether certain structures should actually be discouraged.

If a language to be taught as a national language has
regional colloquial varieties and a prestige variety, it is
quite possible that the prestige form will be chosen, especially if it has a literature which can be considered as a
symbol of national identity.   However, it may have syntactic
structures used in the literature but rarely if ever in the
speech of the 'upper classes' using it.   For example, a
passive construction or a particularly complex form of clause
embedding may be considered more elegant than other possible
syntactic forms.   In such cases, it would seem that the
passive and the complex clause embedding should not be taught,
except perhaps in the senior classes of schools.

It could even be considered appropriate to discourage the
use of certain syntactic structures.   Thus in some languages,
e.g. German, there are rather lengthy adjectival phrase
embeddings before the noun.   They were considered highly
prestigious and are still used in formal writing but if not
handled well can hinder rapid decoding, even by native speakers.
Should such constructions be discouraged?

(e)   *Lexicon*

It is in the field of lexicon that the need for language
planning within a language is most obvious.   For example, in
many languages there is the need for new lexical items for
technical and scientific matters, new political concepts and
so on.

Three main methods have been used:

(a)   To take words from English, in particular, or from
      some other European language, typically the language
      of the former ruling power.   Taking words from such
      languages would include, for example, scientific
      terms of Latin and Greek origin, e.g. *poliklinik*
      (Indonesian).   More everyday words were often
      incorporated during the colonial era, e.g. *bis*
      (Indonesian), 'bus'.

(b)   To make up words or lexical groups from the language
      itself, e.g. Malay:

              tulang   atas   belakang kepala

              bone   upper back   head

      for 'supra-occipital' or a combination like: *kilang*
      adrenal for 'adrenal gland'.

(c) To take items from a 'classical' language which has
     or had influence on the culture and religion of the
     nation, e.g. Sanskrit or Arabic. Thus in Indonesian,
     ilmu bumi 'geography' from Arabic *ilmu* 'knowledge,
     science' and Sanskrit *bumi* 'earth, world'.

Problems of course may occur in some languages because the
phonological system is very different from that of the main
source languages for scientific terms. This problem is discussed by Barnes (1973) in regard to Chinese where there is the
added problem of orthography. Thus, scientific words could be
written in a combination of Chinese characters representing
morphemes having a reasonably similar *sound* to the scientific
name, e.g. à-sz̄-pī-líng 'aspirin', lwó-ji 'logic'. In each
case, the original loan is analyzed into syllabic units, and
then characters with similar sound values are selected to
represent them. Alternatively, the method of transliteration
or *meaning* translation can be used, e.g. má-lì 'horse' and
'power' 'horsepower' or ywán-dž 'original' and 'particle'
'atom'.

We have shown that language treatment in one form or
another concerns speakers of almost all languages. Language
planning concerns speakers of most languages, too, even if only
to the extent that planning is *discussed* even if not acted on.

POINTS FOR DISCUSSION

1. If a language needs new lexical items and
    there are no great phonological problems in
    taking them from English, Latin or Greek,
    for example, are there any valid objections
    to this? Would it be better to make up words
    from norphemes of the language itself?

2. If a language had been written in a script which
    was most unsuitable in regard to its relation
    to the phonology and morphology, what might be
    objections by speakers of the language to a new,
    rational spelling system in Roman letters?

3. What would be objections to a policy of not
    teaching certain syntactic structures which
    were hardly used except in 'classical'
    literature?

4. Would it be feasible to regularize the verbs
    of English? Thus, just as we have the

regular Present - Past/Past Participle forms:
love, loved;   bake, baked, we could have:
break, breaked;   catch, catched, etc.
Children are inclined to do this and say,
for example, *I seed him.*   What objections
would there be to *allowing* such forms and
gradually *teaching* them?

EXERCISES

1.   Make a list of some scientific, technical
      and other new vocabulary recently introduced
      into the language of a new nation.   Is there
      any pattern, for example, in the choice of
      English words, words made up from morphemes
      of the 'native' language or words from another
      'classical' language if there is one?

2.   If the principle of 'one sound - one symbol'
      were carried out for English, investigate
      problems which could occur regarding the
      spelling of any *one* phoneme.

3.   Make a list of the variant spellings used in
      advertising and for trade names, e.g. *Supa-
      Valu* for *Super Value, Kleenex* instead of
      Cleanex, etc.   Can you see a pattern in their
      construction (different letters, fewer letters,
      etc.)?

ASSIGNMENTS

1.   Collect and classify all statements by
      politicians, important figures in the
      community, etc., and all letters to the
      editors of newspapers, weeklies, etc.,
      for a certain period of time regarding
      language treatment.   Is there any particular
      pattern in the particular points raised?

2.   Does the education authority in your area
      lay down rules or guidelines regarding
      'correct' or 'desirable' usage?   Do text-
      books used in the schools do so?   Investigate
      what is prescribed or suggested.   Are there
      contradictions?

3.   Investigate failures in attempts at language

planning or other language treatment.
What were the causes of the failures?
(You may find it appropriate to concentrate
on one case if you can obtain a considerable
amount of information on it.)

RECOMMENDED   READING

Fishman J. A. ed.   1968.   *Readings in the sociology of
language*.   The Hague : Mouton.

Section VII: The Social contexts and consequences of
language planning, contains the articles by Haugen,
previously mentioned and five others.   Section VI also
contains some articles relevant to this area.

Two books specifically about language planning are:

Rubin   J. and B. H. Jernudd eds. 1971.   *Can language be
planned?*   Honolulu : The University Press of Hawaii.

Rubin   J. and R. Shuy eds. 1973.   *Language planning: current
issues and research*.   Washington : Georgetown
University Press.

Both of these books contain articles on various aspects
of language planning.   Some are concerned with language planning theory and some are based on actual
examples of language planning.

10.   THE   MEDIA   IN   A   SOCIOLINGUISTIC   PERSPECTIVE

10.0   *Channel, Receivers and Setting*

There are basically three different types of mass approach
to the public in westernized cultures, i.e. newspapers and
magazines, radio, and television.

Taking Hymes' concept of 'channel', we can distinguish a
marked difference between each type.   Newspapers and magazines
have to rely on the visual aspect, i.e. relaying messages via
written symbols or pictorial images.   Radio uses only the
sound channel which conveys actual speech, noises and music.
In television, one has the most complex array of channel
features, i.e. sound (speech, noises and music) and visual
(pictorial images and at times written symbols).

Although the three forms of the media have different
'channel' features as regards the transmission of the message,
they do have certain similarities too in that they all address
a more or less unknown audience, i.e. all the people who read
the papers, listen to radio or watch television.   The media
have often calculated the *type* of receiver that they wish to
reach but the fact remains that out of individually unknown
groups of receivers (i.e. readers, listeners and viewers) they
have to attract people who will respond to the message - but
respond by acceptance rather than by response.   We wish to
call this group of receivers that is 'appealed to' by the media
for certain reasons and at certain times the *goal receivers* who
should be considered as a subset of the whole group of receivers who are just exposed to the media in one form or another.

It is necessary with regard to media situations to give a
more detailed distinction between *Sender* and *Addressor* than
the one supplied in Chapter 2:

Sender: Either initiates the message or consciously
            modifies its content.

Addressor: Relays the Sender's message (utters it, hands
            it on, writes it out, etc.)   He does not
            purposely modify it but may modify it inadvertently.

Another special feature of the media is that, except for some letters to the editor and radio and TV talk-back programs, there is virtually no dialogue type of communication (special cases will be discussed later).   The message is absorbed and may be accepted but, except for circulation figures and public opinion surveys showing popularity ratings, the reaction of the goal receivers to the messages is somewhat shrouded in mystery.

There is something special about the *setting,* too.   In most cases there are double time and double place components (Platt 1974a).   Exceptions would be, for instance, the immediate radio relay or the live TV show in the same time-zone (single time component).

We shall at first discuss the three forms of media separately and then deal with a special type of media phenomenon, advertising.

10.1   *Newspapers, Journals, etc.*

We shall not go into such problems as whether the reports in a newspaper are written by journalists of that paper or whether they are supplied by a news agency.   Nor shall we deal with matters such as the degree of freedom a journalist has in writing his reports, how much editing takes place, whether in some respects the Senders are the management of the newspaper or even of a large combine of which the newspaper is only a part.   Such problems are quite real and are relevant to the study of radio and television as well but they are beyond the scope of this book.

Basically, in regard to ordinary news items, we can say that the Senders are the journalists representing the newspaper. The Receivers are the reading public.   Thus, for any news item, we can represent this as:

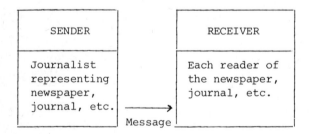

SENDER	RECEIVER
Journalist representing newspaper, journal, etc.	Each reader of the newspaper, journal, etc.

Message

However, there are some special cases, one of which could

be exemplified by the publication in full of an important
policy statement of the Prime Minister (or Leader of the
Opposition, President, etc.).   The Prime Minister would be the
Sender and one might think that was all that needs to be said.
However, although we said the speech is reported *in full,*
decisions have to made such as: Is it to start on page 1?
Are sub-headings to be put in?   Thus, a typical practice is to
give 'highlights' on page 1 and perhaps the full text on pages
4 and 5.   The 'highlights' on page 1 may emphasize less favourable parts of the speech, e.g. inflation, unemployment, whereas
important favourable parts, e.g. new trade deals, social wel-
fare plans, are mentioned only in the full text.   Similarly,
headings and sub-headings such as P.M's GRIM FORECAST may give
a biased impression of the total speech.   We could therefore
say that, although the Prime Minister is the *Primary Sender,*
the journalist(s) could be considered as *Secondary Sender(s)*
and that the message is *filtered* or *distorted* by the Secondary
Sender(s).

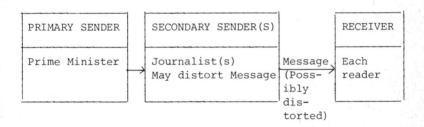

By the way, this is *not* a case of a separate Sender and
Addressor (as when the government's policy is read by the
monarch at the opening session of the British parliament).

The concept of *Goal Receiver* is useful in any discussion
of the media.   Newspapers and magazines are often directed
towards a particular section of the community.   Thus there are
popular (sometimes sensational) newspapers and others directed
at a more limited readership.   There are magazines for women,
brides-to-be, hi-fi enthusiasts and so on.   Within a newspaper,
there are women's pages or sections, children's pages, business
pages, motoring sections and so on.   *All* readers may notice
these sections but it is not *expected* that men will read the
social chit-chat on the women's pages.

An interesting feature of newspapers is the attention
getting device of the headline or caption to a picture.   It is
well known that headlines often reflect the policy of the newspaper, e.g.

TREASURER PRESENTS FAIR SHARES BUDGET

by a paper favourable to the government,

DESPERATE VOTE CATCHING BRIBES IN BUDGET

in an anti-government paper.

Another interesting feature of headlines and captions is that they are almost always based on certain presuppositions. These may be subdivided into:

1. *Temporal* - readers can be expected to understand at that period in time.

2. *Regional* - readers can be expected to understand in the region of the paper's main readership.

3. *Global*   - readers anywhere can be expected to understand (subject to language ability and excluding isolated groups).

4. *Specific* - a sub-group only of readers can be expected to understand.

Some examples are:

1. *Temporal*   CYPRUS DAMAGE $840m

(in August 1974) depended on knowledge of the war there.   It would have made no sense at certain other times.

2. *Regional*   A.L.P. CRITIC MAY BE DISCIPLINED OVER LETTER

Besides the presupposition of *which* critic, there is the regional one regarding A.L.P. (Australian Labor Party) which would be unfamiliar to most readers in other countries. Even more regional would be a headline like:

JONES   RESIGNS

where it is only in a particular country area that *Jones* is recognized as the name of a local councillor.

3. *Global*   In the headline

AIRLINES MAY PUT BEDS IN JUMBOS

there is the global presupposition regarding

Jumbos as large planes, particularly Boeing
747s.

4. *Specific*   A picture of a tiger with a broken leg in
plaster under the caption:

FIRST ROYCE, BARRY AND CO.,
NOW RIJINI'S A TIGER CROCK

would make little sense to anyone not an
enthusiastic follower of Australian Rules
Football who would know that the first two
names refer to members of Richmond football
team (The Tigers) who, along with several
other team-mates had suffered leg injuries
during that football season.

Of course, headlines can be purposely misleading on the
basis of presuppositions. Thus if a headline had:

BLOGGS   RESIGNS

(Bloggs being the name of the Prime Minister) and readers then
found that Bloggs was a little known head of a minor government
department who had resigned they would feel cheated.   However,
there are cases where the headline can suggest more than its
actual denotative meaning, e.g.

PRESIDENT APPOINTS BLONDE TO STAFF

could be true in that the President had done so.   However, the
regional presupposition might be that the public knows that the
President has had various asociations with blondes.

Headlines, like the rest of a newspaper report, may also
play on matters like different connotations of a lexical item.
Thus:

CHILDREN IN CRIMINAL GAOL

could lead readers to think first of quite young children.
Whatever the unpleasant features of the case, it appears that
the eleven juveniles were aged 14 to 17 years.   Although there
may be definitions of child (e.g. legal definitions) as up to
18 or 21, a dictionary definition of childhood is: 'from
birth to puberty' and this accords more with the common concept.

10.2   *Radio*

Type A.   For many programs, e.g. musical, we can consider the
announcer as the sender (and addressor) and the listeners as
the receivers.   Particular announcers and particular stations
could be associated with particular goal receivers in the sense
of sub-groups of listeners, e.g. young people who listen to
certain types of popular music will listen to a particular
station, even to a particular disc jockey.

A subtype of this category would include cases such as
where the Prime Minister speaks to the nation.   It might at
first be thought to be similar to the case mentioned under
Newspapers of a Prime Minister's speech being reported in full.
However, unless there were actual distortion of his spoken
speech by cutting out parts, distorting the sound, etc., the
distortion mentioned previously would not occur.   Thus the
model for Type A would be:

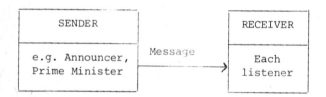

Type B.   A news commentary spoken by a university lecturer or
foreign affairs expert from a newspaper would also fit into
the Type A, Sender = Addressor pattern.   However, a news broad-
cast, for which the news items had been prepared by journalists
but which was read by an announcer would fit into the following
scheme:

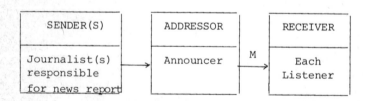

Type C.   This would be the interview type program which will be
discussed under *Television*.

10.3   *Television*

Just as with newspapers and radio, we have the *goal
receivers,* i.e. members of particular age groups, interest
groups or social classes who are appealed to by the media.
In certain cases, we have the TV announcer or TV personality
in impromptu speech as sender/addressor;   in some cases, i.e.
where programs have been specially scripted, we have a sender
(the script writer) and an addressor (the announcer).

TV situations can, however, be far more complex than this.
We should like to deal here in particular with two types:

Type C (the interview situation) and Type D (the
quiz program type of situation).

Situation Type C - The Interview

In this type we can see a 'situation within a situation'.
Let us call them situation c and situation C, where c is a
subset of a larger set C.   Situation c concerns the actual
interview in the studio between, for instance, the interviewing journalist and the interviewee.   Situation c practically
becomes a 'message' that is conveyed (in situation C) by the
TV station (the S-participant) to the goal receiver (the R-
participant) as can be seen in the diagram below:

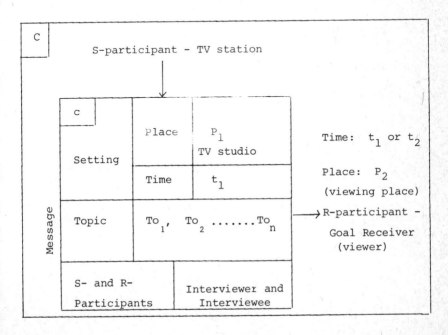

Situation Type D - The Quiz Program and Similar Programs

This type of situation is even more complex than type C because, if there is a studio audience, one has to consider two types of R-participants in situation d as shown in the diagram below:

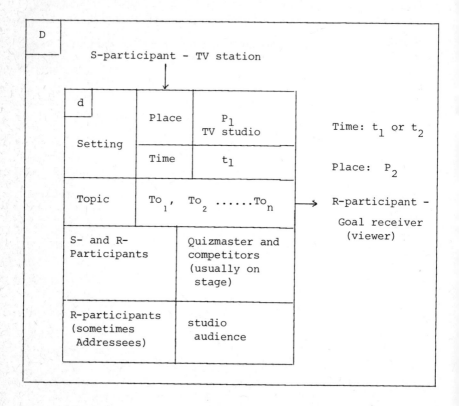

Taking our previous definitions (see Chapter 2) of the S-participant (speaker/sender) as including the concept of Addressor and R-participant (receiver/hearer/audience) as including the concept of Addressee, unless otherwise specified, we can distinguish here between 2 types of R-participants:

Type 1 - The Primary Receiver
          who is an addressee and can also function in the
          speech situation as a speaker/addressor (i.e. the
          quiz master or a competitor in the quiz).

Type 2 - The Secondary Receiver
who is sometimes an addressee (if addressed by the
quizmaster/compere) but rarely functions as a
speaker (i.e. the studio audience).

POINTS FOR DISCUSSION

1. Some types of newspaper situations seem to
have similarities to 'letter situations' and
some types of radio situations show similarities
to 'telephone situations'.   In what way are
these two pairs similar and in what way do they
differ?

2. Discuss the concept of the goal receiver.   Is
is a useful one or not?   Give reasons.

3. Discuss the models of situation types C and D.
Do you agree with them?   Can you suggest other
ways of dealing with these types of situation?

4. Is it useful to distinguish between *Primary*
and *Secondary* Receivers?   Why?   Why not?

10.4   *Newspaper and Magazine Advertising*

The participant structure of newspaper and magazine
advertising is, in general, more complex than that of the non-
advertising content.

In the simplest type of advertisement, there is a direct
appeal to the receiver or at least the goal receiver, for
obviously an advertisement for baby foods is meant to appeal to
mothers rather than the community in general.   However, as the
advertisement appears in a newspaper or magazine and not on the
factory or a shop, we could consider the advertiser as the
Primary Sender and the newspaper or magazine the *Secondary
Sender*.   We shall ignore problems related to how advertising
agencies might fit into the scheme.   Thus the model will be
basically the same as the second model under 10.1.   Although
the newspaper or magazine would hardly purposely distort the
message of one of its advertisers (this, however, is not
impossible), it would have the option of accepting or rejecting
certain advertisements, could even deliberately seek out the
type of advertisement it wished to present, or influence the
way in which advertisements are presented.   It is for these
reasons that we consider the newspaper or magazine a *Sender*
rather than just an *Addressor*.

Some advertisements quite plainly address the reader and have imperative structure, e.g. *Come into our world now* as the main slogan in an advertisement for a chain of motels. Others have a statement heading, e.g. *She never sleeps* advertising a cargo shipping service claimed to have fast turn-around in ports.   However, the advertisement later states: "If your cargo is bound for.... send it by the ships that never sleep...".   Some advertisements include no overt imperative, e.g. for real estate it is common to state the features and price of the property for sale.

The type of newspaper or magazine advertisement in which there is a separation of sender and addressor is not common but is more in evidence in popular newspapers and magazines.   This type of advertisement shows the picture of a person. Often it is someone well-known to the reading public (e.g. a TV personality or a sportsman).   The main caption purports to be the words of the person, e.g. an advertisement for a building society: *I wouldn't save anywhere else!*

Ignoring, for the moment, the distinction between Primary and Secondary Sender, this technique can be represented as

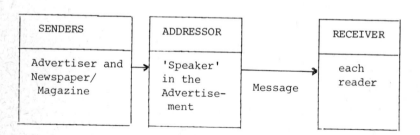

A third technique, not actually very common, is the type where S- and R- participants appear in the actual advertisement. This would include the comic strip type of advertisement. Here we have the same phenomenon as that already discussed under 10.3 *Television* where the message from the Sender to the Goal Receiver is in the form of a speech situation:

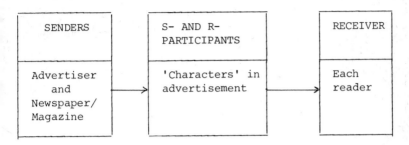

Message
in form of a speech
situation

     The question could be raised whether such 'artificially'
created situations, where the characters utter prepared dia-
logues, can or cannot be classed as proper speech situations
with S- and R- participants.   Of course, there is a whole
continuum of situations ranging from entirely scripted situations (e.g. comic strips, scenes in radio and TV plays and
advertisements, scenes in stage plays and films) through semi-
scripted situations (e.g. TV personalities' shows and some
interview programs) to speech situations where the participants
create their message content and form on the spot (e.g. actual-
ity interviews, and some discussions).   However, for simp-
licity's sake we shall ignore this problem for the moment.

     In the 'situation-within-a-situation' type of advertisement,
the Goal Receiver is usually meant to identify more or less with
the R-participant in the central situation.   This will be
discussed in more detail under 10.6 *TV Advertising*.

10.5   *Radio Advertising*

     Here, the simplest type of advertisement has the adver-
tiser and the radio station as Senders and the person presenting
the advertisement as Addressor.   If he (or she) is a well-
known personality, he (or she) may seem to endorse the goods or
services advertised.   Here, there is not a distortion of the
message of a kind not desired by the sender - as in the case of
arragnement of a verbatim report of a speech in a newspaper but
a *reinforcement* of the message.   We could therefore consider
the advertiser as *Primary Sender,* the station as *Secondary
Sender* and the person presenting the advertisement as *Tertiary
Sender* and *Addressor:*

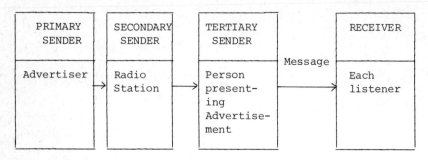

Certain advertisements are, of course, aimed at a sub-section of the community and for these the utterance of the advertisement by a particular personality is important.   Thus, if a woman who runs a daytime talk back program appears to en-dorse a brand of canned food, this will have considerable impact on those women who enjoy this program.

The technique of having an interview situation in an ad-vertisement may also be effective, e.g. if in an advertisement for a car dealer, there is an 'interview' between an interviewer and a 'satisfied' customer, identified by name.   This type of advertisement, where the message appears in the form of a speech situation, fits the second model illustrated under 10.4 *News-paper and Magazine Advertising*.

In radio advertising, too, greater effectiveness is obtained by presupposing knowledge on the part of the Goal Receiver, e.g. an advertisement for a Rock Concert:

> Tickets $5.50 and $4.50 inclusive at the same
> old agencies for .... Concert No. 2
> at Festival Hall, Monday 19th.

'The same old agencies' could be rather meaningless to that section of the community who attended symphony concerts or chamber music recitals.

10.6   *TV Advertising*

As in radio and newspaper advertisements, the roles of Sender and Addressor are often not identical.   The proprietor of a firm may, but rarely does, advertise his own products. We can often consider a *Primary Sender* (the firm or government instrumentality which is advertising), a *Secondary Sender* (the TV station) and an *Addressor* and possibly *Tertiary Sender* (an actor or a TV personality).   Apart from this, TV advertising situations often resemble situations of the C or D type des-

cribed under 10.3 *Television,* where the message is in the form
of a speech situation.

But there are additional factors.   A television commercial
has to be effective, and considering its time span (some last
only a few seconds), it has to achieve its effect quickly, i.e.
to 'brainwash' the goal receiver to buy a certain product or to
carry out a certain action.   The double image of place (p_1 and
p_2) can be a considerable hindrance to the aim of quick and
effective 'brainwashing'.   Therefore, two main approaches are
possible:

(a)   a Place Merger (of p_1 and p_2) and

(b)   a Place and Participant Merger (Platt 1974a).

(a)   *Place Merger*

The simple but less common solution is that Place$_1$ (the
place of the commercial) moves into Place$_2$ (the goal-receiver's
(viewer's) place), e.g.

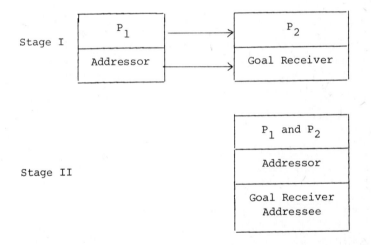

This is possible in such cases where there is only an addressor
(and no addressee) in the commercial and where visual imagery
suggests this process, e.g. in an advertisement for a new type
of canned soup:

Addressor sitting at part of a dining table with the
other part intruding (seemingly) into viewer's room.

In an advertisement for olives:

> Addressor (a well-known cookery expert) talking across
> a bench in a kitchem or family room.

Linguistic strategies aiding this process would be:

   (i)   Direct second person address.

  (ii)   Conversation - where actor takes only one
         interlocutor's part and leaves breaks as
         if a second interlocutor were present.

(b)   *Merger of Places and Participants*

An attempt is made, by visual and verbal (sometimes also
other sound) strategies to merge p_2 (the goal receiver's
(viewer's) place) with p_1 (the place of the commercial) by
forcing the viewer to merge with the image of one of the
participants:

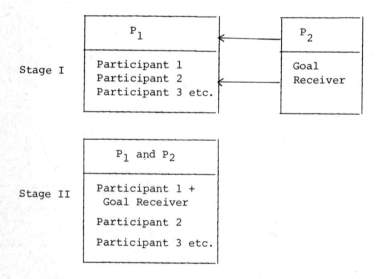

The visual strategies are numerous e.g. only the hands of
one of the participants are showing, only the back of the head,
one participant moving into the frame of the picture from an
outside location, and other more complex devices.

Linguistic devices are often of a rather 'ritual-type'
magnetic nature, e.g. singing, rhyming, repetitions of key word:
easy..... easy..... easy, alliteration of key words, a particu-

lar type of persuasive intonation, etc.

Appeal to Image-Consciousness and Social Class Consciousness

The rugged athlete, the lithe surfie, the tanned bikini-
clad blonde, the sporty type in a racy car or a boat, the
career girl, the soft woman in a floating negligée are just a
few images with which the goal receiver is beckoned to identify
himself or herself.

As far as social class is concerned, there is, for
instance, the immaculately and casually dressed upper-class
gentleman in his leather armchair in his well stocked library
or getting out of his Rolls Royce, the 'jet set' on the terrace
of a luxury hotel in Acapulco or celebrating at a cosy but
expensive ski-chalet.   At the other end of the scale, there is
a deliberate working class image of Ted and Bill in overalls
using X's paper hankies for colds, drinking Y's beer and chewing
Z's chewing gum.

No doubt you can think of many more examples.

POINTS   FOR   DISCUSSION

1.   Do you agree with the concepts of 'Primary'
      'Secondary' and 'Tertiary' Sender as regards
      advertising?   If one wished to include the
      advertising agency too, how could this be
      fitted in?

2.   Why are so many presuppositions made in media
      advertising and in media reporting in general?
      Would it not be better to give more details
      rather than expect a lot of additional knowledge
      on the part of the goal receiver?

3.   Would you consider entirely scripted situations,
      such as scenes from radio or TV plays or scenes
      from stage plays or films, as 'true' speech
      situations?   Do the S-participants (the speakers)
      in these situations really *initiate* the message
      content?

4.   Can you think of any other models which would
      express an effective 'drawing in' of the goal-
      receiver into the central situation?

EXERCISES

1. Show in what way the speech of a minister, government official or other public figure could be distorted by an unscrupulous journalist or newspaper editor.   Give several examples.

2. Take 5 speeches (or statements) by government ministers on a variety of topics and show how they could be reported:

   (a) by a newspaper favourably disposed towards the government;

   (b) by a newspaper which was hostile towards the government.

3. Take 10 headlines and discuss what types of presuppositions are involved in them (i.e. temporal, regional, global, specific).

4. Collect 10 headlines that could be purposely misleading on the basis of their presuppositions and explain why.

5. Classify a number of television programs (**not** advertising programs) into various situation types.

6. Give a number of examples of a radio announcer, TV personality or well-known actor functioning as 'Secondary' or 'Tertiary' Sender.

7. Give some examples of a place merger in TV advertising of the $p_1 \rightarrow p_2$ type.

8. Give some examples of a place merger in TV advertising of the $p_2 \rightarrow p_1$ type (i.e. where the goal receiver becomes one of the participants in the central situation).

ASSIGNMENTS

1. Make a survey of the types of radio stations in your region, the types of receivers they would appeal to and how this is shown by the

speech patterns of their announcers.
(e.g. introducing themselves, introducing
the station, the programs, etc.)

2.   Analyse a number of newspaper advertisements.
     Discuss, for instance, the participants and
     their functions and the presuppositions made
     by the advertiser.

3.   Analyse a number of TV advertisements as to
     place and participant merger, types of
     participants, presuppositions made and
     verbal and visual strategies used by the
     advertisers.

4.   Make a detailed analysis of the linguistic
     and visual strategies used in a group of
     advertisements which appeal to either class
     consciousness or image consciousness or
     both.

RECOMMENDED READING

Although there are a number of books dealing with the
media as such, there are few which deal with it from a linguistic point of view and none, to our knowledge, which has an
overall socio-linguistic approach.

One of the best of the linguistic books on advertising
written in English to date is:

Leech G. N. 1966. *English in advertising: a linguistic
     study of advertising in Great Britain.* London :
     Longmans, Green & Co. Ltd.

11.   PLAYING   WITH   LANGUAGE

11.0   In this chapter we shall consider some uses of language
for humorous and other special effects.   Playing about with
language is a common activity.   Included in this are the
telling of jokes and funny stories, the asking of riddles,
the singing of comic songs and so on.   However, it also
includes all kinds of activities such as making up nonsense
words, giving people nicknames, etc.

It is not our purpose here to try to offer psychological
explanations of humour but to look at a number of types of
'playing with language' from a sociolinguistic viewpoint.
We can first consider phenomena which would not be classed as
jokes.   Sometimes these phenomena are meant to have a
humorous effect but sometimes they may be used to create
attitudes of friendship or solidarity or to show attitudes of
dislike.

11.1   *Nicknames*

A dictionary definition of 'nickname' is 'Name added to
or substituted for person's, place's or thing's proper name,
abbreviation or familiar form of Christian name'.   This is
obviously not sufficient as there are a number of aspects which
have to be considered as well when looking at the concept of
'nickname'.   Apart from the actual structuring principles,
there are also the speaker's attitude to the nichnamed object
as well as the adequacy of the naming, i.e. the nickname has
to be logically acceptable to those knowing the nicknamed
object.

I.   *Naming Procedures*

(1)   *Some structuring principles*

Some examples of nicknames formed on different principles
are:

(a)   Rearrangement of letters of the name, e.g. *Nerts* as a
nickname for a teacher, *Mr. Stern;   Skram* as a nickname

for someone with the surname *Marks*.

(b)   The American practice of referring to people, including
      several presidents, by their initials, e.g. *FDR, LBJ, JFK*.

(c)   Forming a name by reading the initials as a word, e.g.
      Jef (pronounced like Jeff, Geoff.) for someone with the
      initials J.E.F.

(d)   Forms somehow based on the name, e.g. *Ike* for President
      Eisenhower; *Ming*, the first syllable of the Scottish
      pronunciation of the name *Menzies* for a former Australian
      Prime Minister.

(e)   The adding of /iː/, spelt *y* or *ie* to surnames, e.g. *Smithy,
      Jonesy*. The restriction here seems to be: (a) name must
      be monosyllabic, (b) must end in a consonant.

(f)   Rhyme or assonance or some other resemblance, e.g.

             Jim   ⟶   Dim Sin

             Mr. Hausberger   ⟶   Mr. Hamburger

      sometimes with an added element, e.g.

             Mrs. Perry   ⟶   Mrs. Ferry boat.

(g)   Extension of name, e.g. D. Field ⟶ D. Fieldmouse.

(2)   *Speaker's attitude to the nicknamed object*

      Many cases of nicknaming show quite clearly the attitude
that the 'namer' (who is not necessarily the speaker) had when
the name was first used, e.g. *Cuddles, Honeybun* and *Birdie*
would generally suggest a favourable attitude of the speaker/
namer. On the other hand, *Beerguts, Old Misery* and *The
Butcher* would generally be indicative of a negative attitude.

      Prosodic features need to be taken into account as they
often indicate whether the original meaning of the concept is
intended or a reversal of it, e.g. given certain prosodic
features, the following apparently derogatory nicknames could
be used quite affectionately: *Stinker, Faceache, Fatso*.

(3)   *Adequacy of naming*

      As the continued use of a nickname depends to a great
extent on its acceptability by others than the speaker/namer, it
is necessary for a nickname to be to some extent appropriate

for the nicknamed object.

For instance, a very tall, muscular person may be called *Lofty* or (using the technique of opposites) *Shorty*, but *Fatty, Fatso, Tubby* would not be appropriate.

A massive, grim looking university building may be called *Alcatraz* or *The Cottage* but hardly *The Town Hall* or *The City Library*.

II.   *Conditions for Use*

Some nicknames can appropriately be used if the nicknamed person is present or even if such a person is the addressee, e.g.

>   Hullo Shorty.   You comin' fishin' too?

>   I think J.J.B. should be on the committee.
>   (J.J.B. is nearby.)

In other cases, it would be most inappropriate to use the nickname in the presence of the nicknamed person except for the purpose of insult, e.g.

>   Hullo Grumpo.   (to the boss)

>   I think old Skinflint here should pay the next round.

POINTS FOR DISCUSSION

1.   Do you know of any types of nicknaming in other languages?   Are there any particular patterns of nicknaming?   Do these relate to attitudes towards the nicknamed persons or things?

2.   We have given examples of nicknaming of people. Are there patterns of popular names or abbreviated names for *places* in some particular region?

11.2   *Taunts and Rejoinders*

Investigations at a school have shown that taunts occur when someone disliked or despised is approaching, being approached, or is about to speak.   Prosodic factors play a large part in gaining effect.   Loudness and pitch features vary according to whether the taunt is in fun or in earnest.

Typically among boys, a ringleader speaks and the others laugh. Among girls, the practice of grouping together in order to taunt is common.

Taunts such as:

> Order in the court,
> The monkey wants to talk

naturally call for rejoinders. These may be graded from 'weak' to 'turning the tables', e.g.

Be quiet!	is very weak.
Oh, I know you are/do!	turns the tables to some extent but is not particularly effective.
Well all right, start talking!	turns the tables quite well on the taunter(s).

DISCUSSION

Is there some favourite pattern of taunting among children in your area? Do they equate the person(s) taunted with some kinds of animals, do they mention physical disabilities do they use racial or religious taunts or insult the child's relatives?

11.3   *Children's Language Games*

Some examples of rhymes used by children of about 10 at a middle class suburban school to pick out an individual to be 'he' in chasing games are:

(a)   Red top taxi,
       One, two, three,
       Red top taxi,
       You are *he*.

(b)   Chicago train number nine,
       How many miles down the line?

Other phenomena include the spreading of a rhyme throughout the class. This may then be used in such situations as when a teacher is in disfavour with the class. Examples are:

(a)   Hi ho, hi ho,
       It's off to school we go,
       With razor blades and hand grenades,

Hi ho, hi ho.

Hi ho, hi ho,
It's home from school we go,
With teachers' heads and dangling legs,
Hi ho, hi ho,

(b)   In the evening we have fun,
       When the boring day is done.

Such rhymes may then be chanted in the hearing of (or half in
the hearing of) some particular teacher.   Of course, these are
a kind of taunt and similar rhymes could be used in taunting
other children.   (*1).

POINTS FOR DISCUSSION

1.   Remembering your own school days, what kinds
      of rhymes or other verbal devices were used
      in picking 'he' in games?

2.   Why are rhymes used by children to express
      dislike of those in authority?   (Refer to
      observations and discussions in Chapter 3
      concerning Addressee and Listener/Audience).

11.4   *Riddles*

It has been suggested (Roberts and Forman 1972) that
there are relationships between the incidence of riddles and
certain cultural variables such as strong responsibility
training (of children), high political integration, the use of
oaths, and games of strategy.   They also list some cultures
according to riddling:

Definitely having riddles	71
Indeterminate	13
Definitely absent	3
Unreported	110

They mention that in some cultures there are riddling contests.
However, they do not give any classification of riddles themselves nor of the sequencing in riddling (riddle play).

Typically the sequencing of riddles is:

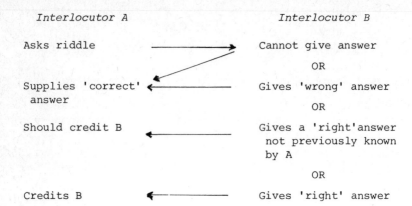

Many classifications of riddles are possible. Some riddle types will be suggested and exemplified. Of course, some riddles may belong to several categories at once.

(a) *Obvious Answer,* e.g.

Q. What goes up when it rains?
A. Umbrellas.

Q. What is a pig after it's three days old?
A. Four days old.

(b) *Double meaning question,* e.g.

Q. How do you stop fish from smelling?
A. Cut off their noses.

(c) *Alphabet riddles,* e.g.

Q. What starts with E and ends with E and has only one letter in it?
A. An envelope.

(d) *Human attribution,* e.g.

Q. Why do mother kangaroos get angry on rainy days?
A. Because their children have to play inside.

These examples will serve to show some of the types but other types occur and other classification criteria are possible.

There are fashions in riddle types, e.g. elephant riddles, moron riddles. There are also fashions in the structuring of riddles. Thus, besides the basic pattern, 'conditional response' types occur, e.g.

Interlocutor A:	What's green, is made of concrete and grows when you water it?
Interlocutor B:	I don't know.
Interlocutor A:	Grass.
Interlocutor B:	But grass isn't made of concrete.
Interlocutor A:	I just put that in to make it hard.

There is also the 'serial' type, popular with 'elephant' riddles. Riddles are asked in a series. The answer to one may appear to help with the answer to the next but is not the acceptable answer, e.g.

Q.   What's the difference between an elephant and a grape?
A.   A grape's purple.

Q.   What did Tarzan say to Jane when they saw the elephants coming over the hill?
A.   The elephants are coming over the hill.

Q.   What did Jane say when she saw the elephants coming over the hill again?
A.   Here come the grapes.   (she was colour blind)

Some other classifications which could be investigated are:

(a)   'Real world' based on linguistic factors versus 'Unreal world'.

(b)   Those which can be *transformed* into a 'one line' joke versus those which cannot.

(c)   In some cultures, children's riddles versus adult riddles.

DISCUSSION

Does the asking of riddles depend on the ages of the two interlocutors? Can both be adults or does one of them have to be a child?

11.5   *Puns*

Of course, riddles may be based on punning, e.g.

Q.   What's the difference between a weasel and a stoat?

A.   One's weasely distinguished and the other ('s totally)
      different.   (stoatally)

Punning sometimes occurs, however, apart from riddles, sometimes
quite spontaneously, e.g. "I can't afford a new car so I'm
Holden on to my old one.   (Holden - General Motors car made in
Australia).   To this, someone could reply: "I can't af*Ford*
one either."   Someone might then add: "Well, you don't want
to be too *Austin*tatious."

     Such strings of three or four attempts at punning form a
kind of game which may continue until the participants can
think of no more puns or someone in the group cries halt.

                  POINTS FOR DISCUSSION

     1.   Someone once said that punning should be
           a punishable offence.   What are the
           attitudes to punning in your community
           (country, town, university or college, 'in'
           group, etc.)?

     2.   What are the makings of a *good* pun?   Does
           it depend only on phonic matters?

11.6   *Verbal duelling*

     A particular type of language play among Turkish boys
from about 8 to 14 is described by Dundes, Leach and Özkök
(1972). They state that this is a genre of oral art found in
many parts of the world.   The authors relate this type of
oral play to features of Turkish culture, particularly the
Turkish world view which is said to be at once fatalistic and
aggressive, to male attitudes to women and to the practice of
circumcision - they feel that this practice - typically per-
formed when the boy is in the four to eight year old range -
has certain psychological effects.

     Basically, the initiator of a 'verbal duel' makes an
insult of a sexual nature and particularly of a homosexual
nature.   The insulted one tries to cap the insult with an even
better one, preferably in rhyme, e.g.

     A.   Ayι
          'bear'

     B.   Sana girsin keman yayi
          'you   enter   violin   bow'

(May the bow of a violin enter your anus.)

Bear is evidently a common insult in Turkey.

Sometimes an innocent question will be met with such a reply, e.g.

A. Hayrola
    'What's going on?'

B. Gotune   girsin   kayrola
    'Ass your to enter let it   bedstead'
    (Stick a bedstead up your ass.)

Sometimes an insult may receive a long and elaborate insulting response, one example given by the authors consisting of 13 lines in: aa, b, c, ddd, ee, ff, gg rhyming scheme!

It appears that a common - and potentially dangerous - practice in the game is to make a verbal phallic attack on the addressee's mother or elder sister.   This may lead to responses which are not purely verbal.

DISCUSSION

Does a kind of verbal duelling occur in your group?   What part does sexual insult play in it?

11.7 *Signifying and Marking*

Two types of verbal play in Black American English are exemplified and discussed by Mitchell-Kernan (1972).   It seems that there are many labels given in Black American English to types of verbal play.   This conscious labelling of types of verbal play by the members of the speech community is common in the Black American community.

A. *Signifying*

An example of signifying is

WIFE   Where are you going?

HUSBAND I'm going to work.

WIFE   (You're wearing) a suit, tie, and white shirt?
         You didn't tell me you got a promotion.

Here, the husband does not normally wear a suit to work.   The wife is suspicious but instead of asking him a direct question she suggests (tongue in cheek) that he has been promoted and is now the sort of person who wears a suit to work.

B.   *Marking*

Marking is a way of retelling a story or incident by parodying features of the voice and mannerisms of the character(s) in it.   Evidently, in Black American English, the oral parody is often uttered in a higher pitch, even falsetto. For example, a pretentious person may be parodied by delivering what purport to be that person's words enunciated very clearly and without normal elisions.

Other strategies appear to include parody of 'Uncle Tom' type speech, as in an example where a black was felt to be siding with management

> "(Drawling) He said, "Ah'm so-o-o happy to be here today.
> First of all, ah want to thank all you good white folks
> for creatin so many opportunities for us niggers and ya'll
> can be sho that as soon as we can git ourselves qualified
> we gon be filin our applications......"

POINTS FOR DISCUSSION

1.   Are you aware of other types of verbal play in
     your speech community?   What are the tech-
     niques employed in them?

2.   Reporting of other people's speech acts is
     typically either (a) in indirect speech or
     (b) in a *parody* of direct speech.   Is this
     true?   Consider speech patterns of men,
     women and children in various social classes.

11.8   *Limericks*

Among some English speaking groups, the telling of limericks is a form of verbal play.   One person will start and others will try to continue in turn.   Sometimes, the limericks may be of a taboo nature and in such cases, each participant may wish to cap the previous limerick.

Limericks follow a strict pattern of rhyme and metre, i.e.

Line	Number of Primary Stresses
1	3
2	3
3	2
4	2
5	3

with the 3 stress lines 1, 2 and 5 rhyming together and the 2 stress lines 3 and 4 rhyming together.   Desirable features include:

(a)   Double (or 'rich') rhymes (or near rhymes), e.g.

   dahlia, failure;   Bosham, wash 'em.

(b)   Place names (or less desirably a person's name) as final words, preferably in the first line, e.g.

   There was a young girl from *Nantucket*
   Who went down a well in a *bucket*

An example incorporating these features is:

   There wás a young gírl from Tóttenham,
   Had no mánners or élse she'd forgótten 'em.
   At téa at the vícars,
   She tóre off her kníckers
   Becaúse, she explaíned, she felt hót in 'em.

Limericking does not have the element of attack on the opponent as the Turkish boys' verbal duelling does, but it provides a kind of folk verse contest.

Verse improvisation occurs in various cultures, sometimes complete improvisation, sometimes the capping of a line or couplet by an appropriate rhyming line or couplet from a store of remembered lines.

DISCUSSION

Are there particular *settings* for certain types of verbal play?   What effect has the number of participants on some types of verbal play?

11.9   *Jokes*

Apart from the psychological implications (which we shall

not discuss here), jokes have many societal aspects.
Linguistic features of jokes are closely related to contextual
features such as ethnic background, sex and age of interlocutors, and also societal attitudes to certain religious and
ethnic groups. We shall discuss only a few of these points.

(1)   *Inter-group jokes*

Phonetic features are closely integrated with attitudes to
certain ethnic groups and appropriateness of situation in the
so-called 'ethnic joke'.

Most speech communities have certain (often only half-
serious) attitudes about stock characteristics of members of
other communities (either other nations or maybe minority groups
of the same community). For instance, in England and Australia: Scots = stingy, Irish = jolly but rather devious, Italian
males = excitable and rather sexy. Many jokes concerning
these groups not only presuppose the listener to have a knowledge of the particular 'ethnic' characteristic and to accept
it but in order to succeed they have to be told with the
appropriate 'accent', i.e. what the speaker considers to be an
approximation of Scottish or Irish English, for example strongly
aspirated stops for Irish jokes and syntactic structures like:
"It's after talkin' to Mrs. Murphy that I was..."

(2)   *Intra-group jokes*

In some speech communities, members of a certain group
will tell jokes about their own group, both in intra-group
situations and to outsiders but it is not always considered
appropriate for outsiders to tell such jokes to members of the
group. In some cases it would just be considered ineffectual
as an outsider would lack the appropriate background and
language structures, e.g. it appears to be true that the most
delightful Jewish jokes are the ones told by Jews about themselves in either Hebrew or Yiddish.

(3)   *Jokes in relation to setting and role relationship.*

Many typical joke situations arise out of what Fishman
(1971) would call *incongruent situations* where either the
setting or the role of one of the participants, or both, are
wrong.

Often jokes involve a person in a certain status position
being found in a setting (in a place, at a particular time)
which is generally considered to be unsuitable for his or her
particular public role, e.g.

a government minister in a strip-tease dive

a leading member of a women's guild taking part
in a Black Magic witches' dance in a churchyard
at midnight.

POINTS FOR DISCUSSION

1. What ethnic (or other) groups are joked about
   in your area?   Are there distinctions on a
   scale of 'kind - unkind' in these jokes
   regarding different groups?

2. Would you say that there is any difference
   between the inter-group and the intra-group
   type of joke?

EXERCISES

1. You may be able to listen to children's verbal
   games.   See whether you can classify them
   according to various features, e.g. where used,
   what participants, what situations, structure
   of the verbal game.

2. Try to think of some taunts and highly effective
   rejoinders to them.

3. *Signifying* and *Marking* are just two kinds of
   verbal play.   If you are able to gather
   examples, try to classify various kinds of
   verbal play.   There may, of course, be no
   special name in your community for these
   activities.

4. Investigate the linguistic content of *ethnic*
   or *religious* jokes.   What are the linguistic
   features (phonetic, lexical, syntactic
   structures) attributed to the group or groups
   which are joked about?

ASSIGNMENTS

1. Make your own classification (with examples)
   of one or more of the following:

(a) nicknames

(b) riddles

(c) puns

2. By the use of suitable questionnaires, try
    to find whether there is a relationship between:
    punning, asking of riddles, telling of limer-
    icks and other kinds of verbal play and age,
    sex and social class. You could ask informants
    to supply puns, riddles, limericks, etc., or
    perhaps better ask them to supply up to 5 of
    each if possible.

RECOMMENDED READING

There does not seem to be much literature available on a
sociolinguistic approach to the types of language play discussed in this chapter.

The following articles give some insight into certain
problems but are of a rather restricted nature.   They are
all in:

Gumperz J. J. and Hymes D. eds. 1972.   *Directions in
        sociolinguistics*.   New York : Holt, Rinehart
        and Winston.

Dundes   A., Leach J. W. and Özkök B.   The strategy of Turkish
        boys' verbal dueling rhymes, 130-160.

Mitchell-Kernan C.   Signifying and marking: two Afro-
        American speech acts, 161-179.

Roberts J. M. and Forman M. L.   Riddles: expressive models
        of interrogation, 180-209.

Footnote

(*1)   J. Jenkin, a senior student in Linguistics at
        Monash University supplied these examples.

APPENDIX: FIELD METHODS

The field of the sociolinguist need not necessarily be the territory of a primitive tribe or a whole urban district. Domains such as the home, college or university, certain areas of employment, the media, all could be objects for fascinating studies.

The writers do not intend to give detailed advice here on statistical methods (there are some good books on introductory statistics available) but rather to give some practical advice, based on experience, on how to go about collecting suitable data in appropriate places without antagonising the informants or anyone else and being sued or arrested for breaking the law.

There are some basic points which should be considered before starting on any exercise or assignment involving field work:

(1) Define your terminology

(2) Define your objectives

(3) Delineate your area of observation

(4) Choose your test persons carefully

(5) Construct suitable tests

(6) Secure suitable recording equipment (if required for the investigation)

(7) Plan a preliminary pilot study (if you are undertaking a larger type of investigation)

(1) Don't take basic sociolinguistic terminology always for granted. As you have seen, some terms may mean different things to different people. Briefly define, if necessary, what you mean by the terminology that is part of the topic of your investigation.

(2) Many students just start off interviewing or recording without having much idea what information they wish to obtain. A suitable area for a study to show up age difference in the use of certain vocabulary would hardly be the workshop of a factory where most employees are aged from 30-40 but rather two different groups, say members of an Elderly Citizens' Club and

members of the 'younger set' of the local tennis club.

The best approach is to make a brief outline first of what information you hope to gather and what significance it *could* have for your investigation.

(3)   There is no need to interview 100 people in order to get the data for an exercise or a small assignment and then to be landed with a mass of data and a nervous breakdown. Work out carefully approximately how many informants would give you the results you are after and stick to that estimate (unless one of the 'snags' occurs which we shall discuss later).

(4)   This is really related to (2) and (3) but refers to 'background' and similar information. If you wish to investigate *English* usage by *native* speakers do *not* include informants who have a foreign background (except as a contrast- ing group). In investigating the speech of a small local area, do not include people who have just recently moved into it, or who may have travelled such a lot that their speech patterns are no longer typical.

(5)   For some types of investigations, testing in a written form could give better results than casual interviews, as you can concentrate on the information you are after. But there are several points to watch:

   (a)   In questionnaire type tests, keep your questions
          brief and adapted to the verbal repertoire of
          your informant(s).

   (b)   In binary-choice and scaling-type tests, make
          sure that your informants are familiar with the
          terms you use. Remember that Tucker and Lambert
          discussed the choice of suitable terms with their
          informant groups first. This may not be possible
          but students have found that for smaller investi-
          gations, a simple range from

          good ⟶ bad   or   used ⟶ used ⟶ used ⟶ used
             (4 degrees)   always sometimes rarely never

          is often more effective than an elaborate array of
          grading terms which may not only be confusing to the
          informants but also time wasting.

(6)   The most suitable recording equipment for a lot of socio- linguistic field work would be a little cassette recorder with a built-in or pop-up microphone. For certain phonetic investi- gations on a bigger scale a high quality cassette or tape

recorder with a separate good quality microphone may be
required.

(7)   For longer investigations, it may pay to do a quick
pilot study to clarify certain factors mentioned under (2) -
(5).   This could be quite informal, observing the use of
language in the street or in interview programs on radio or TV,
asking certain people about their use of some linguistic
features, trying out a questionnaire or a test to see whether
it is suitable.   Relatives and friends are often good,
readily available guinea pigs for certain pilot studies.

The Field Work Itself.

Here again, there are several points to remember:

(1)   How to approach your informants

(2)   How to choose a suitable area for interviewing or
       recording

(3)   The length of time allotted to interviews

(4)   How to deal with other persons indirectly involved
       in your project.

(1)   The degree to which you should take your informants into
your confidence depends very much on the type of results you
are after.   You usually get more genuine results if you leave
your informants in the dark about the matter you are investigating.   This does not mean that you should lie to them - but
often you can give a rather general, slightly vague explanation,
e.g. 'the language spoken in this region' or in interviews
'your opinions on certain topics'.

Show your informants that you are grateful for their co-
operation and for giving up their time to help you.

(2)   Try to get a quiet area where you and the informant
won't be disturbed.   For written tests, it should be well lit,
for recording relatively small to avoid echoing (but not cell-
like) and free from extraneous noise.   This is the ideal
situation which you should strive for but cannot always expect.
The writers had sometimes to contend with echoing board-rooms,
noisy airconditioning, whirling fans and a female informant
clutching her squawking twins.   The worst was probably a school
room with rattling doors and windows which proved to be also a
transit corridor to the boys' washroom.

Sometimes, of course, the locale of interviewing has to be subordinated to the most important factor of all, i.e. having your informant at ease (see remarks under *The Interview Situation*).

Many detribalized Australian Aborigines insist on being interviewed outside their houses sitting on the steps or in the sand surrounded by toddlers and dogs.   Children often feel more at ease in familiar surroundings e.g. schoolrooms or kindergarten play grounds or the family room at home.   Sometimes they will talk more readily if others of the same age group are present.   (This was shown by Labov (1969) when he described different interviews with the 8-year old Black American boy Leon.   The interviewer squatting on the floor munching potato chips with Leon and 8-year old Greg, Leon's best friend, certainly got Leon talking.)

(3)   Try to keep the interview or testing time short in order not to tire the informant unduly.   Lengthy and numerous questionnaires could just result in your informants writing down any odd thing in order to finish.

Recorded interviews of half an hour are usually quite sufficient for you to get the information you want.   Some speakers will certainly say a lot in that time!   Longer interviews will not only tire the informant but also *you*!

(4)   You may need to approach other persons first, before you approach the informants, e.g. parents or teachers of children you wish to interview, employers, government officials.   It could cause a great deal of unpleasantness if you do not obtain their consent.   A courteous but brief thank-you letter afterwards not only makes these people feel appreciated but also assists you if you wish to interview in the same area.

Often, if the informants themselves are inclined to be suspicious and ill at ease, an introduction by a person with whom they are familiar will help to bridge that initial gap of the unknown.   This is particularly important with migrant groups or groups which are in age or social status far removed from the interviewer.

The Interview Situation

(1)   *Put your informants at ease*

Remember that many people are reminded of their school day examinations when asked to fill in tests and may think of the ordeal of a job interview when being interviewed and recorded.

Even reading aloud can be a strain.   Apart from this, there is the initial shyness and nervousness that some people feel when talking to a stranger, particularly if he is not from their familiar group.

Make your informants feel that you are interested in what they have to say - or in the information they supply for your tests or questionnaires - and appear neither as an 'examiner' nor as a 'boss' but just a friendly human being.

(2)   *Don't correct your informants*

If they are filling in a test or questionnaire, this correction could interfere with your results.   If you are conducting a recorded interview, this will certainly spoil your relationship with the informant and may make him or her tongue-tied or surly.

(3)   *Breaking the silence*

Unless an informant is very shy he or she will usually talk quite freely in the right place, to the right person, on the right topic.   Even if you are after a special type of information, it may at times be advisable to let the informant talk about one of his favourite topics first in order to 'break the ice'.   People are more inclined to talk freely on subjects they like and that they can talk about (e.g. jobs, hobbies, parties, holidays).

The most casual speech can be obtained by getting the informant emotionally involved in the subject matter, e.g. telling about an exciting film they have seen, or a TV program.

(4)   *Steer clear of political and religious topics* if possible, unless of course your investigations deal with these areas. People have at times strong views on these matters and you could unwittingly and quite unnecessarily upset your informants.

(5)   *Don't hide the mike!*

In many countries it is illegal to record anyone without their consent.   Although it is very tempting for the linguist to go around with a hidden recorder or to plant a recorder somewhere in order to get 'real casual everyday speech' we feel that it is really inadvisable.   Apart from the actual legal risk you would be taking, there are two further consider-ations.   The first is that people do not like to be tricked, and if you are found out your relationship with that group of people could be seriously damaged.   Recorders 'planted' at

parties or gatherings have often afterwards caused friction
between the participants.   The second reason is a far more
selfish one from your point of view.   In order to carry a
hidden recorder around, you have to disguise it somehow and
you usually muffle the sound.   If you hide it in a room where
there are several people, it has to be somewhere where it
cannot be noticed, i.e. rather a way from the speakers.   Unless
it has an extremely powerful mike and unless the extraneous
noise level is low, which usually isn't the case, all you may
get are muffled, distorted indistinct snippets of speech which
are not really suitable for any analysis.

Collation of material

An undigested mass of data is virtually useless for any
investigation.   If you have planned your procedure well, you
should never be saddled with a bulk of information with which
you cannot cope.   But even if you understand what it's all
about, make sure your readers do too.   Setting out your
findings in tabulated form or diagrams is often the best way
of presenting otherwise rather complex data.

Snags

(1)   An informant does not co-operate, refuses to fill in the
questionnaire, to answer questions, gives you a persistent
'hm, yeah, no' reply instead of speaking more freely.   Don't
persist for too long.   Thank him/her and look for someone else.

(2)   Your recording equipment breaks down (batteries flat,
tape breaks)

    (a)   Take precautions (spare batteries, spare
           cassettes, etc.)

    (b)   If it *does* happen - don't panic!

What you do next depends on the informant.   In some cases
it is better to go on as if nothing has happened - in other
cases it is better to explain and terminate the interview.

Whatever you do - don't break off in midstream and look
lost.

(3)   You cannot get the exact information you are after.

    (a)   Consider changing the topic somewhat to
           enable you to include the information
           you *have* got.

(b)   Remember that even apparent zero-results
       can at times contain information;   e.g.
       the fact that all women in your street
       refuse to tell you their age would probably
       class them all as at least above 25 or 30.

(4)   Everything goes wrong.

       The informan⁺⁻ ⊥re unc⌐-operative.   The tests prove to
be unsuitabl ⌐r the cassette rec⌐ ³⁻r breaks down and, worst
of all, ' ⌐ur results are not what you . ⌐nted in ⌐⌐⌐ ⌐⌐⌐

       **Cheer up!   This can happen to anyone ⌐ ⌐ing ⌐
r ⌐earch and working with such unpredictable ⌐¹eme⌐
⌐eings and electrical equipment.   Consider it s v
experience, note your mistakes (if there were an⌐¹ ⌐
again on another project!**

BIBLIOGRAPHY

As a number of the articles referred to have been published in various journals and collections, we felt it necessary for the purpose of preserving chronological order to quote publications in the following way:

(1962) 1972

Where there is a year in brackets, if refers to the first publication of the article. The second date mentioned refers to the publication which the writers consider to be the most generally available.

Alisjahbana S.T.
        1971   Some planning processes in the development of the Indonesian-Malay language. In *Can language be planned?* J. Rubin and B.H. Jernudd eds., 179-187. Honolulu : The University Press of Hawaii.

Asmah Haji Omar
        1971   Standard language and the standardization of Malay. *Anthropological Linguistics* 13/2.

Austin J.L.
    (1962) 1971   *How to do things with words.* London : Oxford University Press.

Bach E. and Harms R. eds.
        1968   *Universals in linguistic theory.* New York : Holt, Rinehart and Winston.

Bailey B.L.
        1966   *Jamaican creole syntax: a transformational approach.* London : Cambridge University Press.

Bartsch R.
        1973   Gibt es einen sinvollen begriff von linguistischer komplexität. *Zeitschrift für Germanistische Linguistik* 1/1:6-31.

Bernstein B.
        1964   Elaborated and restricted codes: their
                social origins and some consequences.   In
                The ethnography of communication, J.J.
                Gumperz and D. Hymes eds., Washington D.C. :
                American Anthropological Association.
                (Special issue of *American Anthropologist*)

    (1970) 1972   Social class, language and socialization.
                In *Language and social context*, P.P.
                Giglioli ed., 156-178.

Berkowitz L. ed.

Bickerton D.
        1973

        1974

Bloomfield L.
        1933   *Language*.   New York : Holt.

Bock P.K.
        1968   Social structure and language
                In *Readings in the sociology of lang
                J.A. Fishman ed., 212-222.   The Ha
                Mouton.

Brend R.
        1971   Male-female differences in American English
                intonation.   Paper given at 7th Inter-
                national Congress of Phonetic Sciences,
                Montreal, Aug. 22-29, 1971.

Bright W. ed.
        1966   *Sociolinguistics*.   The Hague : Mouton.

Brown R. and Gilman A.
    (1960) 1972   The pronouns of power and solidarity.
                In *Language and social context*, P.P.
                Giglioli ed., 252-281.   Harmondsworth :
                Penguin.

First published 1960 in *Style in language*,
T.A. Sebeok ed., 253-276.   Cambridge,
Mass. : M.I.T. Press.

Cassidy F.G.
    1961   *Jamaica talk, three hundred years of the
English language in Jamaica.*   London :
Macmillan.

    1971   Tracing the pidgin element in Jamaican
Creole.   In *Pidginization and creolization
of languages,* D. Hymes ed., 203-222.
London : Cambridge University Press.

Cassidy F.G. and Le Page R.B.
    1967   *Dictionary of Jamaican English.*   London :
Cambridge University Press.

Chomsky N.
    1957   *Syntactic structures.*   The Hague : Mouton

    1965   *Aspects of the theory of syntax.*
Cambridge, Mass. : M.I.T. Press.

Clyne M.G.
    1967   *Transference and Triggering.*
The Hague : Nijhoff

    1970   Migrant English in Australia.   In *English
Transplanted.*   W.S. Ramson ed., 123-136.
Canberra : Australian National University
Press.

    1972   *Perspectives on language contact.*
Melbourne : Hawthorn Press.

Corder S.P.
    1967   The significance of learners' errors.
IRAL 5:161-170.

D'Ans A.M.
    1968   *Le créole français d'Haiti.*   The Hague :
Mouton.

Day R.R.
    1973   Patterns of variation in copula and tense
in the Hawaiian post-creole continuum.
Working Papers in Linguistics 5/2:
University of Hawaii.

DeCamp D.

1971a   Introduction: The study of pidgin and
         creole languages.   In *Pidginization and
         creolization of languages*, D. Hymes ed.,
         13-45.   London ; Cambridge University
         Press.

1971b   Towards a generative analysis of a post-
         creole speech continuum.   In *Pidginization
         and creolization of languages*, D. Hymes
         ed., 349-370.   London : Cambridge
         University Press.

Dik S.

1975   The semantic representation of manner
         adverbials.   In *Linguistics in the Nether-
         lands 1972-1973*, A. Kraak ed., 1975,
         The Hague : Mouton.

Dillard J. L.

1972   *Black English: its history and usage in
         the United States.*   New York : Random
         House.

Dixon R.M.W.

1971   A method of semantic description.   In
         *Semantics: an interdisciplinary reader
         in philosophy, linguistics and psychology*,
         D. Steinberg and L. Jakobovits eds.,
         436-471.   London : Cambridge University
         Press.

1972   *The Dyirbal language of North Queensland.*
         London : Cambridge University Press.

Dundes A. Leach J.W. and Özkök B.

1972   The strategy of Turkish boys' verbal duel-
         ing rhymes.   In *Directions in socio-
         linguistics*, J.J. Gumperz and D. Hymes eds.,
         130-160.   New York : Holt, Rinehart &
         Winston.

Ehlich K. and Rehbein J.

1972   Zur Konstitution pragmatischer Einheiten
         in einer Institution: Das Speiserestau-
         rant.   In *Linguistische Pragmatik*,
         D. Wunderlich ed., 209-254.   Frankfurt :
         Athenäum Verlag.

Ervin-Tripp S.
  (1969) 1971   Sociolinguistics. In *Advances in the sociology of language I*, J.A. Fishman ed., 15-91. The Hague : Mouton. First published 1969 in *Advances in experimental social psychology 4*. L. Berkowitz ed., 91-165. New York : Academic Press.

         1972   On sociolinguistic rules: alternation and co-occurrence. In *Directions in sociolinguistics*, J.J. Gumperz and D. Hymes eds. 213-250. New York : Holt, Rinehart and Winston.

Fasold R.W.
         1969   Tense and the form *be* in Black English. *Language* 45:763-776.

         1970   Two models of socially significant linguistic variation. *Language* 46:551-563.

         1972   *Tense in Black English: a linguistic and social analysis*. Washington D.C. : Center for Applied Linguistics.

Ferguson C.A.
  (1959) 1972   Diglossia. In *Language and social context*, P.P. Giglioli ed., 232-251. Harmondsworth : Penguin. First published 1959 in *Word* 15:325-340.

Fillmore C. and Langendoen D.R.
         1971   *Studies in linguistic semantics*. New York : Holt, Rinehart and Winston.

Findling J.
         1972   Bilingual need affiliation, future orientation and achievement motivation. In *Advances in the sociology of language II*, J.A. Fishman ed., 150-174. The Hague : Mouton.

Firth J.R.
  (1935) 1957   The technique of semantics. Reprinted in Firth, J.R. *Papers in Linguistics 1934-1951*. London : Oxford University Press.

Fishman J.A.
         1968   *Readings in the sociology of language*. The Hague : Mouton.

1969   National languages and languages of
            wider communication in the developing
            nations. *Anthropological Linguistics*,
            11/4.

1971a   ed. *Advances in the sociology of
            language I*. The Hague : Mouton.

1971b   The Sociology of language: an inter-
            disciplinary social science approach to
            language in society. In *Advances in the
            sociology of language I*. J.A. Fishman
            ed., 217-380. The Hague : Mouton.

1972a   ed. *Advances in the sociology of language
            II*. The Hague : Mouton.

1972b   Domains and the relationship between micro-
            and macrosociolinguistics. In *Directions
            in sociolinguistics,* J. Gumperz and D. Hymes
            eds., 435-453. New York : Holt, Rinehart
            and Winston.

1972c   The relationship between micro-and macro-
            sociolinguistics in the study of who speaks
            what language to whom and when. In
            Sociolinguistics. J.B. Pride and J.
            Holmes eds., 15-32. Harmondsworth :
            Penguin.

1972d   The sociology of language. In *Language
            in social context,* P.P. Giglioli ed.,
            45-58. Harmondsworth : Penguin.

Fishman J.A., Ferguson C.A. and Das Gupta J. eds.
            1968   *Language problems in developing nations*.
            New York : Wiley.

Flader D.
            1972   Pragmatische Aspekte von Werbeslogans.
                    In *Linguistische Pragmatik,* D. Wunderlich
                    ed., 341-376. Frankfurt : Athenäum
                    Verlag.

Frake C.O.
            1968   Lexical origins and semantic structures in
                    Phillipine Creole Spanish. In *Pidgin-
                    ization and creolization of languages,*
                    D. Hymes ed., 223-242. London : Cambridge
                    University Press.

Friedrich P.
        1964   Semantic structure and social structure;
                an instance from Russian.   In
                Explorations in cultural anthropology,
                H. Ward Goodenough ed.   New York : McGraw-
                Hill.

        1966   Structural implications of Russian pro-
                nominal usage.   In *Sociolinguistics*,
                W. Bright ed., 214-253.   The Hague :
                Mouton.

        1972   Social context and semantic feature: the
                Russian pronominal usage.   In *Directions
                in Sociolinguistics*, J.J. Gumperz and
                D. Hymes eds., 270-300.   New York : Holt,
                Rinehart and Winston.

Gallagher C.F.
        1971   Language reform and social modernization in
                Turkey.   In *Can language be planned?*
                J. Rubin and B.H. Jernudd eds., 158-178.
                Honolulu : The University Press.

Giglioli P.P. ed.
        1972   *Language and social context.*   Harmonds-
                worth : Penguin.

Gimson A.C.
        1962   *An introduction to the pronunciation of
                English.*   London : Edward Arnold.

Goodenough W.H. ed.
        1964   *Explorations in cultural anthropology.*
                New York : McGraw-Hill.

Gorden D. and Lakoff G.
        1971   Conversational postulates.   *Papers from
                the Seventh Regional Meeting,* Chicago
                Linguistic Society.   63-84.

Gorman T.P.
        1973   Language allocation and language planning
                in a developing nation.   In *Language
                planning: current issues and research,*
                J. Rubin and R. Shuy eds., 72-87.
                Washington D.C. : Georgetown University
                Press.

Green G.
1968   On *too* and *either*, and not just on *too*
        and *either*, either.   In *Papers from the*
        Fourth Regional Meeting, Chicago Linguistic
        Society.

Greenfield L.
(1970) 1972   Situational measures of normative language
        views.   In *Advances in the sociology of*
        language II,   J.A. Fishman ed., 17-33.
        The Hague : Mouton.
        First published 1970 in *Anthropos*
        65:602-618.

Gumperz J.J.
1961   Speech variation and the study of Indian
        civilization.   *American Anthropologist*,
        63:976-988.

(1962) 1968   Types of linguistic communities.   In
        Readings in the sociology of language,
        J.A. Fishman ed., 460-476.   The Hague :
        Mouton.
        First published in 1962 in *Anthropological*
        Linguistics, 1:28-40.

1964a   Hindi-Punjabi code switching in Delhi.
        In *Proceedings of the International*
        Congress of Linguistics, M. Halle ed.,
        The Hague : Mouton.

1964b   Linguistic and social interaction in two
        communities.   In *The ethnography of*
        communication, J.J. Gumperz and D. Hymes
        eds., 37-53.   Washington D.C. : American
        Anthropological Association.

1966   On the ethnology of linguistic change.
        In *Sociolinguistics*, W. Bright ed., The
        Hague : Mouton.

(1968) 1972   The speech community.   In *Language in*
        social context, P.P. Giglioli ed., 219-231.
        Harmondsworth : Penguin.
        First published in 1968 in *International*
        Encyclopedia of the Social Sciences.
        Macmillan.

Gumperz J.J. and Hymes D. eds.
1964   *The ethnography of communication*.
        Washington D.C.:American Anthropological

Association.

1972   *Directions in Sociolinguistics.*   New York :
        Holt, Rinehart and Winston.

Hall R.A. Jr.
       1955   *Hands off Pidgin English!*   Sydney :
               Pacific Publications

       1966   *Pidgin and creole languages.*   Ithaca :
               Cornell University Press.

Halliday M.A.K.
       1973   *Explorations in the functions of language.*
               London : Edward Arnold.

Halliday M.A.K., McIntosh A. and Strevens P.
       1964   *The linguistic sciences and language
               teaching.*   London : Longmans, Green & Co.

Hammarström U.G.E.
       1966   *Linguistische Einheiten im Rahmen der
               Modernen Sprachwissenschaft.*   Berlin :
               Springer Verlag.

       1975   *Linguistic units and items.*   Berlin :
       (forthcoming)   Springer Verlag.

Haugen E.
       1968   Language planning in modern Norway.   In
               Readings in the sociology of language,
               J.A. Fishman ed., 673-687.   The Hague :
               Mouton.

Hjelmslev L.
       1939   Caractères grammaticaux des langues
               créoles.   Congrès international des
               sciences anthropologiques et ethnologiques,
               compte rendu de la 2ᵉ session, Copenhagen.

Hockett C.F.
       1958   *A course in modern linguistics.*   New
               York : Macmillan.

Hughes E.C.
       1972   The linguistic division of labor in indust-
               rial and urban societies.   In *Advances in
               the sociology of language II,*   J.A.
               Fishman ed., 296-309.   The Hague : Mouton.

Hymes D.
    (1962) 1968   The ethnography of speaking. In
                    Readings in the sociology of language,
                    J.A. Fishman ed., 99-138. The Hague :
                    Mouton. First published 1962 in
                    Anthropology and human behavior, T. Gladwin
                    and W.C. Sturtevant eds., 13-53.
                    Washington D.C. : Anthropological Society
                    of Washington.

            1964a   Introduction: toward ethnographies of
                    communication. In *The ethnography of
                    communication*, J.J. Gumperz and D. Hymes
                    eds., 1-34. Washington D.C. : American
                    Anthropological Association.

            1964b   *Language in culture and society.* New
                    York : Harper and Row.

            1971   *Pidginization and creolization of languages.*
                    London : Cambridge University Press.

            1972a   On communicative competence. In
                    Sociolinguistics, J.B. Pride and J. Holmes
                    eds., 269-293. Harmondsworth : Penguin.

            1972b   Models of the interaction of language and
                    social life. In *Directions in Socio-
                    linguistics*, J.J. Gumperz and D. Hymes
                    eds., 35-71. New York : Holt, Rinehart
                    and Winston.

            1974   *Foundations in sociolinguistics: an
                    ethnographic approach.* Philadelphia :
                    University of Pennsylvania Press.

Inglehart R.F. and Woodward W.
            1972   Language conflicts and the political
                    community. In *Language and social
                    context*, P.P. Giglioli ed., 358-378.
                    Harmondsworth : Penguin.

Jäger S.
            1972   Sprachbarrieren und Kompensatorische
                    Erziehung: Ein bürgerliches Trauerspiel.
                    Linguistische Berichte 19:80-99.

Jernudd B.H.
            1973   Language planning as a type of language
                    treatment. In *Language planning: current
                    issues and research*, J. Rubin and R. Shuy
                    eds., 11-23. Washington D.C. : George-

town University Press.

Jernudd B.H. and Das Gupta J.
        1971   Towards a theory of language planning.
                  In *Can language be planned?*   J. Rubin
                  and B.H. Jernudd eds., 195-215.
                  Honolulu : The University Press of Hawaii.

Jespersen O.
        1922   *Language, its nature, development and
                  origin.*   London : Allen and Unwin.

Jones E.
        1970   Sierra Leone Krio.   In *The English
                  language in West Africa,* J. Spencer ed.
                  London : Longman.

Joos M.
        1968   The isolation of styles.   In *Readings in
                  the sociology of language,* J.A. Fishman
                  ed., 185-191.   The Hague : Mouton.

Katz J.J.
        1967   Recent issues in semantic theory.
                  Foundations of Language.   3:124-194.

Kraak A. ed.
        1975   *Linguistics in the Netherlands 1972-
                  1973.*   The Hague : Mouton.

Kurath H. et al.
        1941   *Linguistic atlas of New England.*
                  Providence R.I. : American Council of
                  Learned Societies.

Labov W.
     (1963) 1972   The social motivation of a sound change.
                  In *Sociolinguistic patterns,* W. Labov ed.,
                  1-42.   Philadelphia : University of
                  Pennsylvania Press.
                  First published in 1963 in *Word* 19:273-309.

             1966   *The social stratification of English in
                  New York City.*   Washington D.C. : Center
                  for Applied Linguistics.

     (1966) 1972   Hypercorrection by the lower middle class
                  as a factor in linguistic change.   In
                  Sociolinguistic patterns, W. Labov, ed.,
                  122-142.   Philadelphia : University of

Pennsylvania Press.
First published 1966 in *Sociolinguistics*,
W. Bright ed.   The Hague : Mouton.

1969   Contraction, deletion, and inherent
         variability of the English copula.
         Language, 45:715-762.

(1969)   1972   The logic of nonstandard English.
                  In *Language and social context*, P.P.
                  Giglioli ed., 179-215.   Harmondsworth :
                  Penguin.   A fuller version of the
                  article can be found in *Georgetown Mono-
                  graphs on Language and Linguistics*,
                  22:1-22 and 26-31.   (1969)

         1972a   Negative attraction and negative concord in
                  English grammar.   *Language*, 48:773-818.

         1972b   *Sociolinguistic Patterns*.   Philadelphia :
                  University of Pennsylvania Press.

         1972c   The isolation of contextual styles.   In
                  Sociolinguistic patterns, W. Labov ed.,
                  70-109.   Philadelphia : University of
                  Pennsylvania Press.

         1972d   The reflection of social processes.   In
                  Sociolinguistic patterns, W. Labov ed.,
                  110-121.   Philadelphia : University of
                  Pennsylvania Press.

Lakoff G.
         1971   The role of deduction in grammar.   In
                  Studies in linguistic semantics.   C.
                  Fillmore and D.T. Langendoen eds., 62-70.
                  New York : Holt, Rinehart and Winston.

Lakoff R.
         1971   If's, and's and but's about conjunction.
                  In *Studies in linguistic semantics*.
                  C. Fillmore and D.T. Langendoen eds., 114-
                  149.   New York : Holt, Rinehart and
                  Winston.

         1973   Language and woman's place.   *Language in
                  Society*, 2:48-80.

Laycock D.
         1970   Pidgin English in New Guinea.   In *English
                  Transported*, W.S. Ramson ed.   Canberra :
                  Australian National University Press.

Leech G.N.
          1966   *English in advertising: a linguistic*
                    study of advertising in Great Britain.
                    London : Longmans, Green and Co.

Lefebvre C.
          1974   Discreteness and the linguistic continuum
                    in Martinique.   *Anthropological Linguist-*
                    ics, 16:47-78.

LePage R.B. ed.
          1961   *Proceedings of the conference on creole*
                    language studies 1959.   London : Macmillan.

LePage, R.B. and DeCamp D.
          1960   *Jamaican Creole.*   London : Macmillan.

Maas U. and Wunderlich D.
          1972   *Pragmatik and Sprachliches Handeln.*
                    Frankfurt : Athenäum Verlag.

McCawley J.
          1968   The role of semantics in a grammar.   In
                    Universals in linguistic theory, E. Bach
                    and R. Harms eds., 125-170.   New York :
                    Holt, Rinehart and Winston.

          1971   Tense and time reference in English.
                    In *Studies in linguistic semantics,*
                    C. Fillmore and D.T. Langendoen eds.,
                    97-113.   New York : Holt, Rinehart and
                    Winston.

McCormack W.
          1960   Social dialects in Sharwar Kannada.   In
                    Linguistic diversity in South Asia,
                    C.A. Ferguson and J.J. Gumperz eds.,
                    IJAL 4/1:79-91.

Metcalf G.
          1938   *Forms of address in Germany (1500-1800).*
                    St. Louis Mo. : Washington University
                    Studies, Language and literature 7.

Mitchell A.G. and Delbridge A.
          1965.   *The speech of Australian adolescents.*
                    Sydney : Angus and Robertson.

Mitchell-Kernan C.
          1972   Signifying and marking: two Afro-
                    American speech acts.   In *Directions
                    in sociolinguistics*, J.J. Gumperz and
                    D. Hymes eds.   161-179.   New York : Holt,
                    Rinehart and Winston.

Mühläusler P.
          1974   New Guinea Pidgin.   *Hemisphere*, 18/6:23-27

Neustupný J.
          1968   Politeness patterns in the system of
                    communication.
                    Paper given at 8th International Congress
                    of Anthropological and Ethnological
                    Sciences, Tokyo and Kyoto, 1968.

          1969   On 'Interpénétration des systèmes linguist-
                    iques' by E. Petrovici.   *Actes du Xe
                    Congrès international des linguistes*, 57.
                    Bucharest : Éditions de l'Académie.

          1970   Basic types of treatment of language
                    problems.   *Linguistic Communications*,
                    1:77-98

Oevermann U.
          1969   Schichtenspezifische Formen des Sprachver-
                    haltens und ihr Einfluss auf die kognitiven
                    Prozesse.   In *Begabung und Lernen*, H. Roth
                    ed. 297-356.   Stuttgart.

Pike K.L.
          1945   *The intonation of American English.*
                    Ann Arbor : University of Michigan Press.

  (1954-60) 1967   *Language in relation to a unified theory of
                    the structure of human behavior.*   (2nd
                    revised edition) The Hague : Mouton

Platt J.T.
          1973   'Outer' or sentence manner adverbials.
                    Paper given at the Linguistic Society of
                    Australia Meeting in Brisbane, August 1973.

          1974a   The TV commercial - visual and illocution-
                    ary strategies in a special type of speech
                    situation.   Paper given at AULLA Confer-
                    ence Adelaide, August 1974.

1974b   Some Aspects of communicative competence
         and the teaching of English as a second
         language. *English in Australia*, 29:13-20.

1975a   "... or what you will". *Hemisphere*,
         19/4:15-18.

1975b   The Singapore English speech continuum and
         its basilect 'Singlish' as a 'creoloid'.
         Anthropological Linguistics, forthcoming.

Polomé E.

1971   The Katanga (Lubumbashi) Swahili Creole.
         In *Pidginization and Creolization of
         languages*. D. Hymes ed., 57-60. London :
         Cambridge University Press.

Pride J.B. and Holmes J. eds.
         1972   *Sociolinguistics*.   Harmondsworth : Penguin.

Ramson W.S. ed.
         1970   *English Transported*.   Canberra : Australian
                 National University Press.

Reinecke J.
         1969   *Language and dialect in Hawaii. A socio-
                 linguistic history to 1935*.   Honolulu :
                 University of Hawaii Press.

Rehbein J.
         1972   Entschuldigungen und Rechtfertigungen.
                 In *Linguistische Pragmatik*, D. Wunderlich
                 ed., 288-317.   Frankfurt : Athenäum
                 Verlag.

Roberts J.M. and Forman M.L.
         1972   Riddles; expressive models of interroga-
                 tion.   In *Directions in sociolinguistics*,
                 J.J. Gumperz and D. Hymes eds., 180-209.
                 New York : Holt, Rinehart and Winston.

Robinson W.P.
         1972   *Language and social behaviour*.   Harmonds-
                 worth : Penguin.

Ross A.S.C. and Moverley A.W.
         1964   *The Pitcairnese language*.   London :
                 Deutsch.

Rubin J.
          1962   Bilingualism in Paraguay.   *Anthropological*
                    Linguistics, 4:52-58.

          1968   Language and education in Paraguay.   In
                    Language problems in developing nations,
                    J.A. Fishman, C. Ferguson and J. Das Gupta
                    eds., 477-488.   New York : Wiley.

Rubin J. and Jernudd B.H. eds.
          1971   *Can language be planned?*   Honolulu : The
                    University Press of Hawaii.

Rubin J. and Shuy R. eds.
          1973   *Language planning:currect issues and*
                    research.   Washington D.C. : Georgetown
                    University Press.

Sacks H., Schegloff E.A. and Jefferson G.
          1974.   A simplest systematics for the organization
                    of turn-taking for conversation.
                    Language, 50:696-735.

Samarin W.J.
          1967   *A grammar of Sango.*   The Hague : Mouton.

          1971   Salient and substantive pidginization.   In
                    Pidginization and creolization of languages,
                    D. Hymes ed., 117-140.   London : Cambridge
                    University Press.

Saussure F. de
          1962   *Cours de linguistique générale.*   Paris :
                    Payot.

          1966   (English translation).   *A course in general*
                    linguistics.   New York : McGraw Hill.

Schegloff E.A.
          1972   Sequencing in conversational openings.   In
                    Directions in Sociolinguistics, J.J. Gumperz
                    and D. Hymes eds., 346-380.   New York :
                    Holt, Rinehart and Winston.

Searle J.R.
     (1965)   1972   What is a speech act?   In *Language and*
                    social context, P.P. Giglioli ed., 136-154.
                    Hardmondsworth : Penguin.
                    First published 1965 in *Philosophy in*
                    America.   M. Black ed., 221-239.   Ithaca :

                    Cornell University Press.

        1969   *Speech acts.*   London : Cambridge University
                Press.

Sebeok T.A.
        1960   ed.   *Style in language.*   Cambridge,
                Mass. : M.I.T. Press.

Shuy R., Wolfram W. and Riley W.K.
        1967   *A study of social dialects in Detroit.*
                Final report, Project 6-1347, Washington
                D.C. : Office of Education.

Silverstein M.
        1972   Chinook Jargon: language contact and the
                problems of multilevel generative systems
                I and II.   *Language* 48:378-406 and 596-625.

Steinberg D.A. and Jakobovits L.A.
        1971   *Semantics: an interdisciplinary reader in
                philosophy, linguistics and psychology.*
                London : Cambridge University Press.

Stewart W.A.
        1968   A sociolinguistic typology for describing
                national multilingualism.   In *Readings in
                the sociology of language,* J.A. Fishman ed.,
                531-545.   The Hague : Mouton.

Trudgill P.
        1972   Sex, covert prestige and linguistic change
                in the urban British English of Norwich.
                Language in Society, I:179-195.

        1974   *The social differentiation of English in
                Norwich.*   London : Cambridge University
                Press.

Tsuzaki S.M.
        1971   Coexistent systems in language variation.
                The case of Hawaiian English.   In
                Pidginization and creolization of languages,
                D. Hymes ed., 327-340.   London : Cambridge
                University Press.

Tucker R.G. and Lambert W.E.
        1972   White and negro listeners' reactions to
                various American English dialects.   In
                Advances in the sociology of language II,

J.A. Fishman ed., 175-184.   The Hague :
Mouton.

Valdman A.
        1967   *Haitian creole basic course P.1.*
                Bloomington, Indiana.

        1971   The language situation in Haiti.   In
                Pidginization and creolization of languages.
                D. Hymes ed., 61-62.   London : Cambridge
                University Press.

Verdoodt A.
        1972   The differential impact of immigrant French.
                In *Advances in the sociology of language II,*
                J.A. Fishman ed., 377-385.   The Hague :
                Mouton.

Voorhoeve J.
        1961   A project for the study of creole language
                history in Surinam.   In *Proceedings of the
                Conference on creole language studies 1959,*
                R.B. LePage ed., 99-106.   London :
                Macmillan.

        1971   Church creole and pagan cult languages.
                In *Pidginization and creolization of
                languages,* D. Hymes ed., 305-315.   London :
                Cambridge University Press.

Weinreich U.
    (1953) 1964   *Languages in Contact.*   The Hague : Mouton.
                First published in 1953 as Number 1 in the
                series 'Publications of the Linguistic
                Circle of New York'.

Whinnom K.
        1956   *Spanish contact vernaculars in the
                Phillipines.*   Hong Kong

Wolfram W.
        1969   *A sociolinguistic description of Detroit
                negro speech.*   Washington D.C. : Center
                for Applied Linguistics.

        1974   The relationship of White Southern speech
                to vernacular Black English.   *Language,*
                50:498-527.

Wunderlich D.

1970   Die Rolle der Pragmatik in der Linguistik.
        Deutschunterricht, 22/4:5-41.

1972a   Sprechakte.   In *Pragmatik und Sprachliches
        Handeln*, U. Maas and D. Wunderlich eds.,
        69-161.   Frankfurt : Athenäum Verlag.

1972b   ed.   *Linguistische Pragmatik*.   Frankfurt :
        Athenäum Verlag.

Wurm S.A.

1964   *Motu and Police Motu: a study in
        typological contrasts*.   Linguistic Circle
        of Canberra Publications, Series A,
        Occasional Papers 4.

1966   Pidgin-a national language.   *New Guinea
        and Australia* 7:49-54.

1970   Pidgins, creoles and lingue franche.
        Linguistics in Oceania, T.A. Sebeok et. al.
        ed. (Current Trends in Linguistics) The
        Hague : Mouton.

INDEX